I WENT TO SCHOOL THAT LONG FOR THIS?!

For more information on Tyler, this book, and random bits that may not have anything to do with either, go to tylerwaye.com

TYLER WAYE

I WENT TO
SCHOOL
THAT LONG
FOR THIS?!

THE REAL CAREER STORY... AND HOW TO CHANGE IT

IN.FORM
Series

Published by IN.FORM Series. Printed in Canada

First edition

IN.FORM Series
4006 Ada Boulevard
Edmonton, AB Canada
T5M 4W5

ISBN - 978-0-9920809-2-1

This book is dedicated, in heart and mind, to many.
But above all else, my wife and parents are deserving of a deeper gratitude.

Great love is an exceptional force; without yours, this book would merely be a dream.

TABLE OF CONTENTS

TRACK 1.
ENTER HERE

This track at a glance: You already know if the career track you're on, or working towards, doesn't feel right. Stop blindly following. This first step is the big one.

I remember it vividly, that Saturday night in June 2006.

Standing on the media catwalk high above the ice surface in Rexall Place, I was looking down on the pregame warm up of the Edmonton Oilers as they prepared to play the Carolina Hurricanes in game six of the National Hockey League Stanley Cup finals. I was yelling as loudly as I could and couldn't hear a single sound I was making. In fact, I couldn't even feel my vocal cords vibrating. It was like standing behind a jet engine and trying to be heard over the ridiculously damaging noise. The sound was literally sucked from me and engulfed by the decibels filling the air. It was absolutely fantastic.

You see, the Edmonton Oilers Hockey Club was in the play-offs, and not only that, the team had made it to the final possible home game of a Cinderella playoff run. The city was electric. There were endless parties. Nobody could think about work. Cars were driving around with 10-foot oil rigs mounted on their roofs. Grandmothers were high-fiving each other in the street. And here I was, a twenty-five-year-old sports fan, born and raised in Edmonton and now working for the team that was the centre of the universe. It would be like working for the Dallas Cowboys during Super Bowl week, or Manchester United leading up to the Premier League final. It was thrilling – magical, even.

Yet, while watching the game we won four to nothing, sending the series to game seven, I found myself shaking my head in disbelief; I would be leaving this job in less than two weeks. What was I doing? Was this job not good enough? Was I seriously looking for something more? Well, yes I was. Of course, standing above a sold-out crowd at a game where people were paying a thousand bucks for a nosebleed seat was thrilling… and most of my friends would say I had the coolest job they could think of. But it just wasn't going to be for me, and I knew I had to move forward in a different way. I was looking to really value and enjoy my life's work, and what I was doing didn't feel right.

The (common) problem

You see, I'd started my career excited by the prospects of work, but was quickly shaken by the reality. Judging from those around me, I wasn't alone. Work wasn't what I'd expected. This was fine; I was ready to learn and grow. However, I wasn't confident how and where to actually start making that happen. I didn't like what I was doing and I was uncertain of where it was leading. It was a bad combination, one I found most troubling. Sure, the challenge and solution seemed obvious – find something exciting about work and bear down – but plans and reality were disconnected. And, I knew that every additional step I took in the wrong direction was making it that much harder for me to recalibrate the way I hoped. Yet, every day I'd wake up and take another blind step towards a future I had little faith in.

Work had only just started, and I was already unsure about the way it was playing out.

You could say my growing sense of career unease was a gut feeling, but there was much more to it than that. After struggling with my entry into work and watching my friends and colleagues suffer similar fates, I'd begun to look for information about successfully transitioning from school to work. A little desperate, I know, but I was panicking. I thought I'd be good at work. I never expected dejection. So, I began looking for quick solutions… anything, really. At first I didn't find much. In fact, I found so little rational and valid information on the topic that in an act of full-on desperation, I wrote to about one hundred of North America's corporate leaders (Fortune 500 sorts). My question: How do you become a rising star in an organization?

Dozens wrote back, and these were the top CEOs and vice presidents from some of the continent's largest companies. My first taste of progress! Their advice was wise: it reflected age-old truisms that included a blend of their personal observations and experiences. This advice provided a thoughtful snapshot of the best they could offer from their perspective, looking back from on high. Of course, I was living a different reality. Sure, they had good insight, but it's fair to say that their vantage point was a little different from mine. And from the bottom rung of the ladder, what I was seeing and experiencing convinced me that there was much more to learn about the gloomy story I was seeing so many people live out.

Even with the input from CEOs, I knew there was still a vast section of missing advice that was needed to help people transition from school to work, a critical time in anyone's life journey. The evidence was mounting: more and more of the people I encountered were just like me, stumbling through the start of their careers.

I began to believe that the story of life had a missing chapter. I was becoming passionate about figuring out what should be in it, even if it meant I had to write it myself.

Why do so many people end up in a job they can't stand?

That is what I would name the elusive chapter. As this seemed to me to be a dreadful situation to be avoided at all costs, it followed that others – people in workplaces and schools – would be interested in the same topic. The conversation simply needed to start.

Without the right information, young university and college graduates continue to enter their careers not realizing they are arriving into a big freaking abyss that very few figure out how to navigate. Without compass in-hand or knowledge of their new surroundings, new graduates walk aimlessly for a period, stumble, retrace their steps, and then move in any direction the wind blows because they don't know what else to do. They're lemmings, moving towards a career future that doesn't have the ending for which they are vaguely hoping.

The lemmings

Does every graduate suffer this fate? No, of course not. But a staggering percentage do. In 2010, *Time* magazine published a report stating that only 45% of Americans are satisfied with their job. In a 2011 report, Gallup (a leading research firm) indicated that 73% of American workers are not engaged or are actively disengaged at work. I was shaping up to be one of them even before I had gotten my career feet wet. So, somewhere along my march into the unknown I stopped in a moment of clarity and thought, "What the hell am I doing? Am I prepared to end up wherever this autopilot path takes me?" I knew the answer to that. I would not walk down that path the majority still take even though it only works out, fulfillment-wise, for a surprising few. I suddenly thought, "The fact that so many people do is crazy!"

What struck me in particular – and still does to this day – is the number of young graduates who get jobs, mentally struggle with their new reality, switch jobs, then get disheartened and stay on a random career path for a few years, never quite feeling comfortable. Then, after finally realizing they want to do something else, they don't because they feel handcuffed to the path they're already on. It's a predictable pattern, a terrible shame, and deserving of a serious warning. I'll argue it's worth much more than that, too.

The amount of energy, effort, and innovation that the collective workforce loses to disengaged workers is absurd. Of this, there is little debate. Yet, based on my investigation into early career issues, it seems that the people who are truly concerned about solving this enormous problem have blinders on and only declare how big the issue is for organizations who suffer this drain. They wonder what might be if organizations could only tap into this unused potential. They worry solely about the impact on business. And, of course, the impact on business is huge! Game-changingly huge. Business is suffering because people become lifeless at work.

But, this is the wrong issue to focus on. The true disgrace is not the effect this drain is having on business; it's the effect this drain is having on the lives of people. People who were unable to get their career feet underneath themselves quickly enough. People who live out entire lives, swayed drastically by the early career choices they made and going through their careers like zombies because they were never truly shaken out of their rut.

What has become clear

As a result of my investigation into the transition from school to work, what's become clear is this: the entrance into work is broken. Youth unemployment numbers throughout much of the Western world are at record-breaking highs; and a 2009 study by Leadership IQ, a research and management-consulting firm based in Washington D.C., pointed out that almost half of newly hired employees will be deemed failures within the first eighteen months of starting their job.

This means that such new hires will be fired, leave under pressure, receive disciplinary action, or get significantly negative performance reviews. A study by the Adecco Group claims that the majority of workers will end up wanting to choose a new career path, if only they could. Yet, young graduates continue to enter work, follow a path that is working out for surprisingly few, and then become disheartened when work fails to live up to expectations.

The game is up. Old, useless career advice needs to be exposed for what it is, and a new approach to career entry needs to be championed. The emerging workforce is waiting. You are waiting. Answers are needed. You are becoming aware of how the path you are on is not leading where you hope. The time for this message is now.

A shift of mind

This book is intended to change the common view because I fundamentally believe that the choices we make from our late teens to our mid-twenties greatly (and gravely) affect our lives in terms of finances, fulfillment, health, happiness, etc. As well, although these early life choices have a mega impact on the rest of our lives, we are poorly prepared to make them. I also believe that people should get a straight shot at being truly happy and fulfilled with work. And, I believe that many others feel the same way but don't know how to create that reality. That's why it's time for this issue to be properly addressed.

You see, the world of work is evolving drastically. There is a rapidly growing group of fed-up people... wanting a life where work complements and supports what they believe to be important. Wanting more control. Wanting to work at something they enjoy doing. Wanting to feel like they're getting good at something that makes a positive difference.

But here's the problem: the current model of work is not helping people find the light. Worker unhappiness is at an incredible high. Careers are drifting further and further from what people actually want. And, young workers entering their career know this; they have seen the writing on the wall. They don't want to follow in the same footsteps if it continues to lead where they have watched it lead. They are scared to death of being stuck in a job they can't stand for forty years.

That's why you are finding yourself in a unique situation. You are not interested in finding success if it means sacrificing life to do so. Also, you have little interest in simply disengaging from work in order to live the life you truly want after hours. So you're stuck because the career challenge you face has two parts. The first part is that you want to find your footing at work. You're keen to get yourself into a position that feels right. You want to succeed.

The second part of the challenge is that you are looking to create a new career path for yourself, one that does not force you to choose between life and work. What you want out of work is something that lines up with who you want to be. You don't want the traditional version of success, not if it requires you to sacrifice the things you value most.

It may sound like a far-off dream, but it need not be. However, the impetus for the changes you envision must come from you. The traditional career path won't guide you where you want to go, nor can a bumbling start to your career continue for long. A shift of mind is needed.

Hope vs. action

So, you can either continue to pray that the stars will align, arbitrarily delivering the career you dream of (a long shot), or you can start taking a more active role in shaping your own career path. If you're not one to leave things up to chance, then the earlier you start the better. I say this because many workers are now coming to realize that many of the middle and late career struggles people face can be directly linked back to their early career decisions. Yet, those who are in a position to guide, coach, and teach the emerging workforce are still not giving young workers the right type of help with the decisions these young workers face. It's ridiculous. A lot of strain is being felt, and with this strain comes career fallout. Therefore, it's time to alleviate some of the pressure.

With a little corrective action, the career you are looking for will not only be a hopeful vision. With new knowledge and resolve, creating this reality in your working life is plausible, even predictable.

So where do we begin?

First, I ask you to shake off a number of assumptions you may hold. These are assumptions many of us blindly cling to because we have failed to imagine what work could look like if we took control of our own path. It wasn't until I questioned my longstanding beliefs about work that things for me really started to change. It's time you give it some thought, so let's critically evaluate if work needs to continue looking the way you have known it. Here's just a taste; many critical evaluations will follow. Deep down, do you believe, like many others, that:

1. Work is to be endured until you can retire as early as possible.

2. Success brings with it a bigger paycheque but only at the expense of your life outside of work.

3. You were successful at school, so you should be successful in your career.

4. Work is simply a means to an end.

5. You could do more, help more, achieve more if only the opportunity was presented to you.

I've come to slowly understand that each of these major (and limiting) assumptions is patently untrue. The following tracks will offer proof of this, but more importantly than that, the changes you will see by deconstructing your beliefs about work – and your actions at work – will become all the proof you need.

So, what began as a poignant and self-centred pursuit almost a decade ago to deeply understand why so many people struggle in their transition from school to work has taken shape in the following pages. The project has been a worthy foe, and rightfully so. There are no cookie-cutter answers to the troubles people experience during the first few years of their careers. It seems you can't untangle early missteps very easily. That's why it continues to be the case that while a few people find their way on the traditional "right track", the rest flounder. Also, those flounder-ers continue to act out a few predictable early career responses that subsequently lead them to lose faith in the potential of their life's work. To put it mildly, it's a trend that would be nice to reverse.

Truth be told, seeing this early career pattern was easy. Finding an alternative has proven to be much more difficult. It's required much more than hopeful theories. For until recently, the "right career track" that people hoped to stumble across seemed to only come about as a result of divine inspiration or luck. That crapshoot path was the best career carrot people were being offered. People still clamour for it; that's why so many people continue to cling to poorly supported hopes. They want the damn carrot! Maybe they still believe like I used to, that the fastest up the ladder wins, that career success takes shape in dollars, titles, and command. It's the reason we continue to allow a system of work to operate that allows a select few to get the carrot while most don't. It's now time to question if there isn't a better way. Shouldn't we change the carrot? No doubt, we should.

Where are we heading?

This conversation we're starting is inspired by an expanding pursuit and objective I call Career Design. It follows on the heels of other lifestyle-centric movements, but adds a touch of – let's call it – security. Career Design is a new path into work and it's based on the premise that your career can and should be carefully shaped to maximize its returns on your quality of life. It's about life and work fitting together, and the doors that become opened are irresistible. I suggest it's a pursuit worth starting.

Career Design is the light on the not-too-distant horizon… it's not a mirage; people are reaching it. These people are the pioneers of Career Design, the ones creating and testing the new model of work. Their patterns of behaviour do not fit the traditional career mould. To them, success has taken on a new look. No longer is it about becoming CEO or vice-president just because. It's lifestyle first, and that requires careful balance. They aren't necessarily in a race to the top-floor corner office, although many of them have the skills to get there. However, they're choosing personal commitment and control over blind organizational allegiance. This is how they are finding a way to stay inspired by work. It's also why they drive to get better and better at something unique rather than allow their career to zoom further out of focus and further out of their control.

Through this approach, they are becoming the new philosophers of work. They are changing the way the game is being played. So, smash the traditional career mould you've been hanging onto. This journey is to rewire your approach to work. It's deeply personal, and well worth the voyage.

Your first choice

Keep reading or shelve the book. It's your call… your first choice. But I'll tell you: the intent is pure. The goal is to facilitate your learning about you and about the most important elements in your life to acquire through work. Don't allow yourself to get distracted. There are many ways forward in life and there are many final destinations. You just need to find yours. It doesn't result from one single change. The recalibration is the result of a series of explorations and shifts that will begin to pull you in a new direction. That's what we're beginning.

If you're feeling career-lost, fret not. If your career has been a series of stops and starts, a new path will emerge. And, if you have yet to start your career, some critical questions and an investigation into some of your most enduring assumptions will be raised.

As you sit with this book in your hands, or displayed on your e-reader, tablet, or some other device, the decision to keep reading and the situation you face in your career journey are unique to you. I won't assume to know your circumstances. However, the deal I offer is this: the final product of your career is yours to make and this book will provide you with a map. It's not the only map, but it's a good one. The career destination it outlines is one that is built on clarity and with modern-day principles of lifestyle in mind. Whether it's the map for you is your decision.

However, regardless of whether or not it traces your road step-by-step, it will serve to illuminate vast sections of terrain that are most likely dark to you now. So, if you're in need of career focus, read the book. If you have yet to embark on your career, read the book. And, if you have never quite found the footing you desire in your career, read the book. Do not despair. You will start to enjoy the ride.

READ ME – Backtracks

Before you truly get going, it's important that I offer the instructions for this book. Chapters are not called chapters; they're tracks. This isn't a story you're reading, it's a process for change. I have offered the tracks in the order that makes best sense to me, but how you ultimately decide to read the following pages is yours to discover. Read and repeat as needed.

As well, I strongly suggest you read one track a day – no more, no less. The tracks are designed to be efficient but they each cover a big topic, one that you will want to let sink in. Trying to blast through the book like a novel will ensure you miss the most important lesson: to discover how all of this applies in your life.

Finally, each track will be laid out in a format like this one. There will be an introduction to a concept, then the explanation of the philosophy or principle behind it. Following that, the end of each track will offer a "backtrack." These backtracks are where the message is drilled home, offering the final piece to discovering how the track is/can/should be played out in your career. So, I strongly suggest you read these backtracks. The questions they ask are key.

And that's it. Buckle down. Read a track a day and allow me to open a whole new vantage regarding work.

TRACK 2.
THE BRICK WALL:
MAN THAT HURTS!

At a glance: You, like almost half of new
employees, may hit the wall. Don't panic; it's to
be expected. The recovery is what matters.

Imagine you've just started your career. For many of you, that will not be very difficult.

You graduated, threw out some résumés, landed your first career job, and you're excited. Rightfully so. It's now time to start doing the very thing you believed you were preparing for – your life's work. You have the best of intentions. It's going to be awesome.

Yet within a short time of starting your job, something feels wrong. You can't quite put your finger on it, but it's definitely there. Something about work doesn't quite feel right. And although you didn't really know what you expected from work, you're certain it wasn't this.

As a result, you start mentally drifting from your job. You have trouble pouring your energy into your work the way you thought you would or believed you could. You are not outright failing; you still handle your day-to-day routine just fine (maybe because your job is really quite simple). But, you've lost your excitement and bad habits are setting in. You are not working the way you should because you cannot figure out how to drum up the desire, every day, when you know the fire just isn't in you. And even though you are aware, to an agonizing level, that you're straddling a great divide with one foot in and one foot out of a career that has only just begun, you are unable to flick the effort switch. Why? Well, that's the troubling part: you've got no clue.

You're fundamentally torn and you are driving yourself crazy. You've got a decent job and you should be thankful. Actually, you are thankful… but only to a point. You start wondering what else is out there; perhaps a different job, more schooling, or maybe you just need some time to collect your thoughts. You are looking at all options. Meanwhile, self-doubt creeps in and grows. You wonder if you just don't have it in you. Maybe you are not willing to work as hard as you thought you would. Or maybe, just maybe, work sucks, and your career is going to become the thing you feared most – a daily toil that simply supplies a paycheque.

Although you're not yet sure about any of this, one thing you're painfully aware of is that the longer you straddle the divide, the more likely it becomes that work will continue to suck. It's as though you've hit a brick wall.

But, you still have hope.

You're not ready to fall into the slow career slide just yet; you want to right the ship. You still envision a career that is based on something you like to do; something that excites you. And you know you need encouraging thoughts in your head, not restrictive ones. What you don't want to entertain – what you're unwilling to contemplate for a second – is that you're living proof that you are unable to handle work or find success. You know both these things are untrue. However, you decide it's time to start getting some answers.

Like I said: maybe you didn't need to think very hard to imagine this scenario.

Early warning signs

The early career storyline you just read is a common one; I know that spot. There's a good chance you do too. But rest assured, the second half of that career story has yet to be written. There are beacons of light out there that can help alter a career path that is starting like this. So if that story feels like yours, or if you're determined not to let it be yours, focus in. What comes first is to get sincerely acquainted with the career entry challenge you face (that we all face). This challenge throws a knockout punch.

The truth about career entry

I think it's best to preface the remainder of this book in the following way:

The 2009 Leadership IQ study monitored the progress of 20,000 newly hired employees as they entered their positions. What Leadership IQ discovered was that 46 percent of those workers (about 9,200 of them) failed at their jobs within the first eighteen months of employment. And by 'fail' it meant fired, left under pressure, received disciplinary action, or had significantly negative performance reviews. It's not a pretty statistic and might I remind you that this study was conducted during the height of the recession, a time when you'd think most people would want to keep their jobs.

How can this be possible?

The results of the study are quite telling. Of the 9,200 employees who failed at their jobs, only 11% did so because of technical incompetence. The rest – the other 89% – struggled because of behavioural factors. They knew what to do and how to do it; their behaviour just got in the way. They weren't idiots or poorly trained, rather they were uncoachable, they lacked social skills, they failed to stay motivated, or they had the 'wrong temperament'. How extraordinary! 8,100 of 20,000 newly hired employees failed at their jobs because they were unable to behave the right way at work.

Now, here's the deal: there are two ways you can interpret this study. The first is to allow the findings to bolster the argument that the emerging workforce is feeling and acting out a sense of entitlement; they are entering work without the conviction they need to work hard and succeed; they are unprepared to accept the responsibilities of professional life. That's the prevalent (and powerful) opinion of the emerging workforce, the standard reaction whenever people hear about the issue of young workers. That's the first interpretation of the study.

Maybe this is true. Maybe today's emerging workforce is that screwed up. If it walks like a duck and talks like a duck… right? Like I said, this is one perspective. However, there is another way to interpret the Leadership IQ study, which I now ask you to consider.

The alternative perspective towards this study is based on the belief that the emerging workforce is struggling with work not because of entitlement issues, but because of preparatory ones: Young workers are failing in their behaviour because they are unprepared for what to expect and they are unprepared for what they will encounter. Furthermore, once they get acquainted with their new work reality they may not like what they see, so they act out. This is the second perspective, and it is a much different way of interpreting the failure of 8,000+ newly hired employees. Potentially, it's a perspective that appreciates the layered depths of the career entry challenge to a greater degree. Maybe this is the perspective that sees the situation with blinders off.

Drawing the line in the sand

The findings of the Leadership IQ study perfectly illustrate two schools of existing thought on the issue of entry level employees' struggles. These different beliefs form somewhat of a continental divide on the subject. Most view it one way, an overshadowed minority sees it the other. The entitlement argument is winning.

For the sake of your progress at work, it's important that you think through where you personally stand on the issue. Is the struggle many people face when entering their careers a work ethic and entitlement issue, or is it the result of poor preparation that is showing up as differing values, choices, and expectations? Most likely you can guess what side of the line I've declared my loyalty to: the side that believes new workers are unprepared for the nature of work. It is the side that also believes that many are not pleased with what they are experiencing in the current system of employment, so they are unwilling to fully commit. That is what I believe, but you need to make up your own mind.

Entitlement or misplaced preparation: It's a critical difference. Yet, as much as the two root causes of the issue differ, the symptoms of both problems look awfully similar. That's why it's easy to mistake one problem for the other. It's also the reason why, when it comes to solving the problem, the opinion-makers have allowed themselves to get led astray. They are misdiagnosing, and their misdiagnosis has become a sincere problem. You see, if the career entry symptoms are misinterpreted, which I believe they are, the mega-problem people face when entering work only intensifies. This means the gap grows wider and wider between your efforts at school and the reality of work.

However, if we can collectively get the diagnosis right, a clearer path to resolution begins to emerge. This is based on the belief that the right diagnosis would lead to the right questions, which would then lead to the proper solutions. This is the way to get the systems of school and work to blur the lines of separation that are causing these two worlds to differ so drastically and screw things up so badly. If only we could diagnose correctly. A lot hangs in the balance.

Unfortunately, according to the Leadership IQ study, balance has not been found. Too many new employees are still having trouble adjusting. Opinions and solutions lay too far in one direction – the direction that sees fault, not promise. The overwhelming belief is that the emerging workforce is simply encountering one of the major growing pains in life and the tough love they are finally experiencing is needed. It's the common conviction, one I am sure you've heard.

Don't let yourself be drowned out if you see things in a different light. It's time for you to diagnose the problem yourself. The majority is loud, no doubt. But if you look and listen hard, you will begin uncovering a different story. And maybe, just maybe, the scales of opinion are beginning to tip. But, like I said, you need to determine on which side of the line you stand.

Tipping the scales

In recent years, as turnover and career entry troubles have continued to mount, organizations have been making efforts to fix the problem (remember, 46% of newly hired employees are failing. This is a big, costly problem). Therefore, the goal has been to slow down the percentage of new employees who get hired and then screw up. To reach this goal, great attention has been focused by employers into better integrating recently hired employees into the true nature of their new role.

Employers are doing this because the belief is that employees decide to stay or go within the first six months of starting their new job. So, if an organization can do a better job of assimilating new employees within the first six months, perhaps more of their workers can be convinced to stay. As well, if the employee can be convinced to willingly stay, maybe the organization can reduce the negative fallout that will inevitably develop, both individually and organizationally, if the employee simply disengages from their job. It makes sense.

Of course, this employee introduction stuff (orientation and onboarding) has been around for a long time; I'm writing of nothing new. The only distinct difference in the efforts of some organizations today is that the workplace intro is no longer seen to just be about shaking hands and picking up a scan card; it's now about getting employees integrated into the culture, processes, and production of work in a much more sophisticated way.

Organizations that understand the true impact of high employee turnover are doing this innovative orientation stuff because they believe if they can reduce the culture shock for new employees, they can improve employee retention. But, they want to test if they're right. They want to ensure the effort and money spent on more thoroughly orienting new employees is worth it.

What have we learned?

Numerous studies have been undertaken to discover if the cost of this new type of employee introduction is worth the expense. The results have been extensively one-sided. Overwhelmingly, employers are discovering that purposefully designed workplace introductions – strategic onboarding – are improving their employee retention, engagement, and role effectiveness. It's a landslide.

Aberdeen, a company that conducts research related to a whole slew of workplace affairs, started testing the results of strategic onboarding efforts in 2006 (right before the recession hit, when employee turnover was most severe). Since that time, following the rise and fall of the recession, Aberdeen has continued to publish reports on the subject. Time after time, their studies continue to find that organizations that better introduce employees to the true nature of their work greatly reduce new employee turnover.

Is that a shocking revelation? Of course not. Most of us would have assumed the same thing. It's not rocket-science stuff. However, the interesting thing is not that employee retention improved. This book is not a soapbox for the improvement of orientation processes (although it wouldn't hurt if those changes occurred). It doesn't matter why retention improved, only that it did.

If young employees were struggling with the transition from school to work because of a sense of entitlement and a lack of work ethic, there would be no significant reason why better onboarding reduces turnover... but it does. Young employees are not unwilling to work, they've simply been struggling to find their footing. It's not a generational flaw, it's a systemic one. Young workers are technically sound; we know this. Remember, of the 9,200 employees who failed, only 11% did so for technical reasons. The missing link is behaviour.

The Aberdeen studies tell us that if we help young employees understand and believe in the behaviours that are expected in the workplace, failure is greatly reduced. These would not be the findings if the emerging workforce simply didn't care. They do. They just don't know what to expect or how to fit themselves into their new role at work. New employees need to get comfortable with where work is leading them. But that's not happening yet. The issue young people face when entering work is not an entitlement issue, it is a preparatory one.

Therefore, we'll spend our time fixing the real issue, not the 'popular' issue that others are wrongly leading us to believe is true. Now let's figure out what all of this means for you.

First things first

Start by thinking about that Leadership IQ study for a moment. Forty-six percent of newly hired employees fail. That is a big number. Huge! It offers a reason to be wary of taking your first few steps into any job. Nobody starts work with the interest of failing, but we still do. So it begs the question: Why are almost half of all newly hired workers failing?

That answer is a long one. Why young workers fail in today's world makes up the next five tracks you will be reading. Pretty soon, you will be well-acquainted with the breadth of issues faced. But before we go there, something else needs to be explained first. Before you know why people fail, it is important to know when they fail (or at least when the failure starts).

The wall

The "brick wall" is the name I've given a person's initial stunning confrontation with early career struggles, frustration and possibly despair. It refers to the period of time when work – or at least your enjoyment of it – comes to a grinding halt and you can't see a way forward. It has adopted this name because people tend to hit it hard. There is a good chance you have already been there. If not, most likely it is on the horizon.

Now, the concept of the brick wall is not groundbreaking. You already know that the entrance into work is broken. I've just given the moment it breaks a name. Statistics indicating that so many newly hired employees fail, or that youth unemployment is at record-breaking highs, or that the majority of workers end up struggling with their career choice don't shock you. You are aware that the transition into work is not working well for many people. Yet, you may not be aware of how the cold, hard problem is truly showing up, and when. That's why this brick wall concept is a necessary piece of the puzzle that needs to be quickly fitted into place.

Bill O'Brien, legendary CEO of Hanover Insurance, said it best:

> *People enter business as bright, well-educated, high-energy people, full of energy and the desire to make a difference. By*

the time they are 30, a few are on the fast track and the rest
'put in their time' to do what matters to them on weekends.

He was exactly right. People are full of enthusiasm when they enter work, yet within a few years they are either finding success or merely putting in their time. Think about that. Within a few short years of starting work, people begin to divide towards success or away from it. So the million-dollar question is: What causes this split? What causes people to go down one of these two paths?

Well, the causes are many. That is why the coming tracks will describe and diagnose exactly why the split has formed. But, I can tell you exactly what marks the beginning of the split. It is the shattering moment when you hit the brick wall. That moment initiates the rift. The brick wall is the time when the reality of work shakes your belief of what you hoped was to come. Consequentially, the notion is a central concept in this book. A ground zero of sorts. Therefore, let's make sure the term is clearly defined. There is no point starting out with misconceptions.

This is how I describe the brick wall:

The brick wall is the hard, painful thing young workers
run into early in their career when they realize work
is not what they expected. It's the thing that sucks air
from sails, leaving young workers directionless, frus-
trated, and unsure of how to proceed. It's the fork in
the road that marks the split towards success or a career
that's defined by simply going through the motions.

That's the brick wall. In essence, if we boiled this entire book down to a simple pursuit, it would be to recognize that the brick wall exists, reduce its impact, and help you fall on the right side of it so that you stay interested in pursuing meaningful work. Then, the book intends to help you design what that meaningful work looks like.

This book aims at the fix for the split. The real fix.

Don't worry! If you've already hit the wall, the fix still works. If you have yet to hit it, all the better; you have time to get prepared in the right way.

Getting led astray

We go to school for so many years (especially for the final few), and we have one primary goal in mind. That goal is to learn, to study, and to prepare to enter our careers. We literally spend years and years increasing our knowledge and our skills for this next step. That's why it's unfortunate that after so much time and preparation, many of us will initially do so poorly at the very thing we are preparing for. It makes you wonder what the driving force behind school has been all along. Frustration is a fair emotion, especially because you are now becoming aware of how early career missteps caused by uncertainty and incorrect preparation are starting young workers down a path that can be very difficult to recover from.

Yet, what many fail to recognize is that the early career missteps people make are not their very first steps into work. The problem is not the doorway itself. Rather, it's what occurs after the door is opened. The true missteps happen after the brick wall is hit.

It's also important to mention that when many people hear of the brick wall, they mistakenly assume that the early career struggles people experience and the reason they hit the wall are because of some calamitous event or major oversight. They couldn't be further off. It's simply not true. Calamitous events are not the cause. Instead, people hit the wall because of a series of subtle yet powerful forces that are causing work to shift in a considerable way. They hit the wall because the environment of work has changed drastically, but no one has told the people who are entering their careers. I wish the problem was as acute as a tangible event, but it's not. The problem is wide; that is what makes it so difficult to avoid.

So, when I said that the world of work has changed and gaps have formed, this is what I meant. It's these new gaps in the working world that are causing people to hit the wall. The problem is that these gaps are very difficult to eliminate. However, like I said, it's not the gaps you should be focused on. You will hit the wall; almost all of us do. It's your reaction to hitting it that will either keep you on track or lead you astray. Remember, the brick wall only marks a moment; it is not the true problem. It marks our ground zero. Therefore, our focus during this book will be on minimizing the damage the brick wall inflicts. This will require one part 'heads up' and one part fast recovery. The process will be introduced through a mix of philosophy, how-to, practical wisdom, experimentation, and grit. The picture this process paints will gradually come into focus.

Remember

As demoralizing as hitting the brick wall is, don't let it overly concern you. As mentioned, most likely even with this heads-up, you will catch a piece of brick. Therefore, the important factor is the recovery: How will you influence the way you split from the fork? Will you hit the wall and get stopped in your tracks, or find a way to overcome?

You have the opportunity to fight for yourself and declare how you will move forward. You can decide to be someone who will design their career future to fit the life they are seeking. Or, you can allow your career to unfold according to the hands of fate, wherever that may lead. As always, the choice is yours.

So, keep your chin up if you have already hit the wall, your eyes up if you haven't. Don't let the wall knock aside a good career because you neglected to understand the situation you faced.

Backtracks

The point of this book is to help you transition into the type of career you are really yearning for. To get there you need to understand the moment that potentially knocks you off track. That is the brick wall.

Now that you understand the wall – seeing it for what it is – our gaze will move elsewhere, as the true problem (the causes, not the symptoms) is altogether different. Therefore, the next five tracks will uncover and explain the powerful forces that are causing the brick wall to rise up in your career. But we are not there yet, and don't let this moment pass you by. The brick wall concept is fresh in your mind. Before you learn about how the brick wall develops, simply understand that it does.

Question 1.   *How do you diagnose the career entry issue?   Is it preparatory or generational?*

Question 2.   *What did the brick wall feel like when you hit it?   If you have yet to hit it, what does it look like, looming out there on the horizon?*

TRACK 3. DISLOCATED: THAT WAS THE RIVER, THIS IS THE SEA

At a glance: School and work don't line up. Not like you thought they did. Discover the gap, then bridge it yourself.

Dr. Karen Arnold of Boston College has spent a substantial portion of her career studying the trajectory of students leaving high school, entering college, and then making their way in their respective careers. Her driving question: can we predict success based on educational background? She has made some telling discoveries. This is one.

In 1981, the Valedictorian Study was launched by Arnold

and her colleague, Terry Denny. The study was developed to follow the lives of high academic achievers, not just through college but for the long haul. It began in Illinois, where 81 individuals who graduated high school as valedictorians, salutatorians, or top honours students were identified and tracked. These were the absolute top-mark students coming out of high school. Off they went to schools around the nation to pursue whatever path unfolded for them.

These students were then closely monitored for over a dozen years. Numerous elements were observed, including colleges attended, grades, graduation rates, marital status, number of children, final educational achievements, and career developments. Promotions were tracked, career choices were monitored, and the impact work had on the lives of these super-achieving students was closely watched. So, what were the findings?

This statement says it best. According to Arnold, "Even though valedictorians are identified as the best in their schools, the result is that almost all end with respectable but not prominent careers." This means that on average, these students went on to good but not 'number one in their class' careers. They didn't follow the trajectory they seemed to have launched in high school. What can we conclude? Simple...

Pulling back the curtain

If you live in a highly developed country, your success at school is not a good predictor of traditional career success. It's just not. Those who do well at school are not necessarily going to do well at work. And there is good reason for this.

Work is fundamentally different than school. An overly obvious statement, yes, but don't gloss over it. As much as we acknowledge that school and work are very different things, most of us fail to recognize how drastically the two differ. Failing to recognize this is a mistake, a very big mistake.

Lack of recognition is causing young employees to assume and believe they can work the same way they did in school, believing all will be okay even though they are in completely different surroundings. They fail to realize that a new approach is required. Consequentially, when it comes to the brick wall forming in your career and stopping you in your tracks, this is powerful force number one. That's why this track is dedicated to clearly differentiating the nature of school and the nature of work.

This difference will matter to you regardless of where you currently stand. I say this because if you're still a student, this track will help you start to discover how school and work fail to line up. As a result, it may change the way you view the coming choices you face. On the flip side, if you're already in your career, you will be asked to embrace the notion that in order to succeed, you need to break the habits you formed at school. Many of those habits were formed to help you progress in a system that is foreign to the world of work you are operating in now, and these habits are doing nothing but holding you back. It's time to take off the shackles.

A tale of two worlds

In the context of Career Design (the new approach to work that will be discussed in future tracks), understanding the difference between school and work is a crucial step. It's crucial because in a subconscious way, most students assume that where school leaves off, work begins. They believe the purpose of school was to prepare them for work, that the exit steps from school drop you at the foot of the path for work with many of the tools you already need in your belt. Although this is the way school is sold to us, it's absolute crap.

For most people, the preparation school offers is foundational. It's not workplace-specific, and it is even further from being entry level workplace-specific. So if you are still clinging to the belief that the skills formed at school are the same skills you need when you start working, get over it. This is an assumption that must be questioned. With Career Design, you must become serious about finding a way to acquire the true skills you'll need for your slice of work. Unfortunately, many of these skills are not being acquired through your traditional education.

Professions and trades aside, school and work have very little to do with each other. One comes before the other, sure. They may also discuss similar topics, creating a vague connection, but other than that they're unrelated. But just because the propaganda suggests otherwise, that doesn't make the reality any less true. Arnold's Valedictorian Study should not be surprising. Good grades in school do not equal career success, and career success does not stem from success at school.

You may have already had this hunch and Dr. Arnold just proved the point. After you graduate, more changes than you may have thought. The world of work rises up to destroy many of the lessons you learned late in your educational journey, perhaps making you question the value of school. And like everything in life, it's worth questioning.

However, tread carefully with these thoughts because regardless of the gap between school and work, school still matters. It matters a lot. Maybe just in different ways than you thought. School has great value; the reasons are numerous. Without question, school is one of the best platforms to explore the things you like, different people, your style of learning, and the fields you may wish to pursue. It's the playground for a lot of the maturation people need to go through. I am a fan of school! Yet, the educational system is far from perfect. School is not the great primer of productive life many hope it to be. And grades, well, they're just not a good predictor of what is to come. School and work, in many ways, just don't sync up.

So what we must gather from the difference between school and work is that in order to build the skills at school that you need to succeed at work, you must seek out that development on your own. As well, in order to succeed at work you must continue learning how to operate according to the new world you now belong to. It sounds disordered. In many ways it is. But focus your fight. Become curious, not disgruntled.

Ask why: That's a good place to start

Before we move forward with our comparison of school and work, it's fair for you to voice your questions. Actually, imperative. For instance, why is it that being good at school – getting good grades – does not mean that you will excel at work? What else were grades grading? And what's the purpose of school if not to line you up with a career?

Soon you'll be able to answer those questions for yourself. The answers stem from the concept you are growing to appreciate, that school and work represent two distinct hemispheres in life. When school was developed, especially post-secondary, the original purpose was far from the pursuit of career preparation, and not enough has changed. That's why grades don't predict success: school and work form two independent ecosystems that share little more than a common border.

These ecosystems operate by two different codes of rules, functioning in two vastly different ways. So as much as we yearn to draw a straighter parallel between the two, it doesn't exist. At least, not right now it doesn't. And it's not necessarily because one system is broken and the other isn't. At least, that's not the conclusion based on this circumstance alone. Rather, it's a case where the left and right hands are more worried about doing their own thing than they are at trying to get better at what they're supposed to be doing together. Therefore, if your goal is to find early career success, if your goal is to reduce the impact the brick wall will have in your world, then your first step must be to appreciate the significant gap that exists between school and work. Then, find a way to bridge this gap.

Be your own mastermind. Sure, the surroundings are new. It makes bridging the gap hard, but that's only hard, not impossible. You've been dislocated from one system and thrown into another. You knew it was happening, but you may not have understood it like this.

That was the river, this is the sea

A number of years ago, I was watching a great surfing film: Riding Giants. A tip to those interested in renting it or Googling it: descriptive clarity is key if the movie store has an eighteen-plus section or your search settings are low-security. Yes, I found that out the hard way, back when we still rented movies. Anyways, Riding Giants is a documentary style film on the origins of surfing and the awe-inspiring lure of the big wave. It's a film that sheds light, in no uncertain terms, about the power of doing what you love. Watch it. Whether you like surfing or not, it's worth an hour and a half of your time.

When I first saw the film, I was sitting there after it finished watching the credits and a song came on as the names of those involved in the film filed past. The title of the song was This is the Sea by a motley crew band I had never heard of called "The Waterboys."

It's a good song, worth a listen, but that's not why I mention it. Rather, it's because of a line in the song that keeps repeating over and over in a pulsing sort of way. At first you're not quite sure how you feel about the repetition, but soon it pulls you in. The line? "That was the river, this is the sea." While I listened to that line sung time and time again, I started to think about the ideas floating in my head about the transition to work, and that line soon became the perfect analogy for describing the journey we all face when leaving school and entering our careers. That was the river, this is the sea. It's the best way I can describe the comparison.

The river

You see, the education system is set up for one purpose. At least in theory it is. It is set up with the goal of educating our youth and preparing them for life. It's a universal pursuit.

The U.S. Department of Education states it this way:

To promote student achievement and prepara-
tion for global competitiveness by fostering educa-
tional excellence and ensuring equal access.

The Japanese think of it this way:

Education shall aim for the full development of personality
and strive to nurture the citizens, sound in mind and body,
who are imbued with the qualities necessary for those who
form a peaceful and democratic state and society. (Ministry of
Education, Culture, Sports, Science and Technology – Japan)

Of course cultural differences play their part, but you could take just about any of the countries in the world and find great similarities between the pursuit of their educational systems. Around the globe, educational goals are very comparable. Now, whether you believe school systems pursue their goals in proper fashion or not is yours to decide, but the agenda of everyone involved is designed to be the same. The focus is to naturally guide students through a journey of development and growth. And whether you go to school in the U.S., China, Sierra Leone or Spain, the nature of the journey that everyone travels looks remarkably similar.

In this way, school is a river. It's a linear and protected pursuit. Progress is uniform and the destination is clear, but the analogy runs even deeper than that. In school, all students move at the same speed and the direction has been pre-determined. Whether you try your hardest or not, the educational system will do all it can to sweep you downstream. You may leave school at a different time than someone else, of course. Yet for a good number of years all will have travelled downstream at the same pace. It's the nature of a river and it's the nature of school.

As any river does not go on forever, nor does school. Inevitably, the horizon will change one day. Prepared or not, the mouth of the river appears. School concludes, and when it does, forward progress takes on a whole new approach and your world is irreversibly changed. What worked before as a means of progress doesn't work anymore; an entirely different strategy is required. You have left school and entered work.

The sea

Just like school is the river, work is the sea. School is sheltered; work isn't. The river is confined. The sea is forever big and just like in work, the boundaries are few. A sea is liberating and overpowering at the same time. And as interested as you may be to explore, the lack of specific direction or guidance seems foreign. Some take to this new world immediately, but many don't. Some require time to adjust. So, although a few look like they know exactly where they're headed from the start, most will need to splash about for some time in search of their bearings. It's inevitable. The pattern becomes predictable because the entry into work, as much as you saw it coming, is a turbulent time. You have come from one system and entered a very different one. That was the river, this is the sea.

From the mouth

School has a guiding hand that directs your progress. It's the last time in life you will experience this type of compulsory advancement. After school is done, no longer will you be naturally advanced just because a year has passed. The working world does not provide this type of inherent progress. To advance at work, you need to provide good reason. This is because work was not designed for your sake. It is not worried about leaving you behind.

On the flip side, school had your best intentions in mind; your development was their core purpose. Work couldn't be more opposite. Although many enlightened organizations see a great connection between the personal development of their employees and the successful achievement of their mission, this is not the norm. For the majority of organizations, the focus is fully elsewhere. Your work has a pursuit that is very distinct from your growth. And, the world of work doesn't care if you get lost in its expanse. Staying pointed in the right direction is your responsibility. At work, unless you provide reason to have someone nudge you back in line or find a way to stay true to a direction you've declared, it's easy to get sidetracked. You must choose your own path and be prepared to deal with whatever it throws your way. The natural direction is unpredictable.

Of course, school has its ups and downs too. You're aware of that. You may get caught up for a short time, but it will ultimately spit you out. You may get bounced around, but you will eventually get through one way or another. By design, it's the way that rivers and our education system work; what starts at the top will make its way downstream. And in large part, this is a wonderful thing. The key, however, is to not let this gentle compulsory progression lull you to sleep, for it will end. At some point the upstream pressure will dissipate. School will end, work begins, and you quickly recognize that now there are no banks on either side for reassurance. Work does not escort you towards your goals unless you move towards them yourself. That's why work without a plan feels aimless.

For all school offers, it only allows you to explore so far. The banks are always there to keep you aiming downstream. This is a double-edged sword. School will rarely provide you the venue to go after what truly interests you. Why do you think Mark Zuckerberg and Bill Gates cut the educational cord? School's designed to guide and teach, but not to allow you to choose your own path, create your own way. Work is just the opposite. It is endlessly big, and it's very easy to get lost. It's also impossible to navigate without making a few mistakes, plotting a course, and developing your own sense of initiative. Work provides freedom and choice, much more so than school, and these elements make all the difference in being able to find fulfillment. That's why work is the ideal platform to share your interests and pursue a unique path. It is a large piece of the fabric of life.

Bridging the gap

That was the river, this is the sea. In this way we can clearly see that while school leads to the mouth of work, the two systems don't align. They are simply two distinct entities in the progression of life. As much as we want them to fit hand in glove, they don't. School has value, but that value must be tempered. It is not providing all the tools you need at work. On the flip side, work may not provide those tools either. Although the world of work offers a fantastic opportunity to pursue whatever you want to in life, many of the tools you need to help you find that path weren't taught at school and weren't offered to you through work. It's a great irony. There is a set of skills and behaviours that neither school nor work will intrinsically teach you. But yet, these skills and behaviours are so badly needed to create a successful career. That's why they need to be developed on your own. Don't worry, we're heading there.

Always connected but fundamentally different

Upon entering work, you will be thrust into a new world that operates in a profoundly different way from school. And the change goes beyond the obvious. It will be more comprehensive than what we learned in the Valedictorian Study, that good marks do not equal a good job. The change permeates just about every crevice of the new system of work you are asked to explore for yourself. However, as big as the transition is from school to work, it need not leave you floundering. Leaving the well-worn and nurturing path of the river to the wide-open expanse of the sea can be one of the best opportunities you are provided in life.

As you continue to take steps forward, know that there is room for you to explore a new way to proceed. In fact, it's necessary. It's also fair to say that you don't yet have a full handle on the potential you can realize through work. You can't: the system is too new and too big. So don't feel restricted, and don't feel overwhelmed.

Backtracks

School and work don't line up. Not like you thought they did. They aim in different directions, providing two very different results. Consequentially, there is a new set of skills that must be mastered to succeed at work. Developing those skills is the pursuit of future tracks. However, for now, all that is necessary is to comprehend the size of the gap from school to work, and why it is leaving people floundering. This gap is the first force that causes your brick wall to develop.

You have left the river and entered the sea. Turbulence and sputtering are to be expected. Staying stuck and battered against the shore is what you must fight. Taking direction for yourself is the way out.

Question 3.   *What do you think school taught you that is creating problems for you now?*

Question 4.   *To overcome those problems, what behaviours and skills do you need to further develop?*

TRACK 4.
HOW ABOUT
THAT FOR TIMING?
THE EVOLUTION
OF WORK

At a glance: You are entering the workforce at a time of historical change. Flat out, work is very different today than ever before.

Referencing work in his 2011 State of the Union Address, President Obama said, "The rules have changed." Yes, Mr. Obama, they certainly have. Work is evolving.

Now, this may not sound like news because you hear

words like this often, but our world has changed fundamentally in recent times and is continuing to change faster than
ever before. Economies are changing, countries are changing,
weather is changing. Yeah, yeah, yeah: you've heard it all
before. However, there is another change afoot that you may
not be aware of. It's a shift that's often overlooked, or worse,
failed to even be recognized. Yet it's no less important to the
way in which you live your life. It is the evolution of the very
fabric of work.

Make no mistake. What work looks like, how we do it, and
what it's offering back to us in return is changing. It's moving
fast. And while the other major changes continue to grab headlines, we'll focus on the forgotten one – the shift that's happening
in offices, organizations, and homes across much of the world.
It's the evolution of work and a progression of culture that is
only beginning to show the magnitude of effect it will have on a
global scale. Without a doubt, it will affect you significantly in
the coming decade. It's already started.

Don't fight it

When I offer that there are several major dynamics you must
be aware of as you launch your career and design how it takes
shape, the evolution of work is on the forefront, vital to understand. It is the second powerful force that causes the brick wall
to rise up in your career, and its importance to you is big because
the heavy handed message it offers is that as work changes, you
must change with it. The alternative is to be left behind, as so
many people are.

This is a fate to be avoided. If history has shown us anything,
it is that those who try to cling to an outdated model of work
when the world changes around them have trouble recovering.

Michel de Montaigne, renowned writer from the French
Renaissance, said it best in his elegant yet cutting style:
"Stubborn and ardent clinging to one's opinion is the best proof
of stupidity." A little harsh, yes, but that doesn't make him

wrong. That's why the suggestion is to be on the leading edge of the shift. To do that, however, it's necessary that you have a firm grasp of the changes occurring in the world of work. They are things that may be difficult to immediately see from your vantage, but are no less real to you and no less consequential.

If the evolution of work sounds like a situation that falls outside of the scope of your control, if it feels too big to factor into your plans, rethink it. The term work is not a static term. It's a living, breathing action that bends and moulds with the circumstances of the day. You've grown up seeing it look a certain way, but that look is changing. And, it just so happens we're living in a time and place in which many of the world's historical shackles are being shattered, so the look of work may start to change faster than you anticipate. Therefore, as much as the last track described how important it is to understand the transition you're making from the system of school to the system of work, you now need to factor in that the system of work itself is in flux.

Whether we embrace it or not, short of global economic collapse (bigger than we have already seen) there is no way to stop the full-speed charge into the next frontier of work. We can't fight it; we simply need to be fast learners. Failing to understand and accept the new way the world operates could lead many to career implosion. In certain ways, and in certain areas, we're already seeing this occur.

Change breeds what?

It may sound scary, and in all fairness, it is. We are entering an unknown frontier complete with considerable uncertainty during which the main models of work as we've known them will change. This will be a tough pill for some to swallow. But it's not all bad news. The flip side of the coin is a shiny silver lining to workplace uncertainty: that is, opportunity. The generation currently entering the workforce, known as Generation Y (you), will have unprecedented opportunities because of that uncertainty. You're being forced to deal with this uncertainty, but you gain opportunity back in return. In this way, the situation is divisive. The workplace you're entering will provide some people with unparalleled prospects for personally ideal levels of fulfillment, finances and freedom, the likes of which we've never seen. But as the changes in the work world continue to roll on, the ups and downs will leave just as many in the ditch that runs alongside.

While that has a huge upside, your downside could look just as steep. Understandable. The catch is that because of the time and place in which you live, you are required to give up considerable security. In return, at least, you gain choice and a better chance at controlling your own fate (if you're willing to take hold of it). Is it a fair trade? Only time will tell.

What we know, however, is this: while some people currently starting their careers will create new definitions and levels of success, many others will be left to a career full of confusion, disruption, and/or mind-numbing years spent doing things they don't care about, all the while knowing that things could have been different had they made different choices earlier on. The former sounds thrilling; the latter, tormenting. And for those who fall into the distressing situation, most likely it won't be because of a lack of desire or capability to succeed. Rather, it will be because they simply won't know how to shift with the times. They'll be swallowed up in the wake of the evolution of work. It's the reality of our time.

A brief (rudimentary) history of work

You may find this interesting.

Modern humans, as we would recognize ourselves, first emerged about 200,000 years ago, give or take and depending on the reference. These first people lived on the continent of Africa before snaking their way along the coasts of today's Middle East, India, Burma, Thailand, Malaysia, Indonesia, and parts of Australia. The migration was not fast, it took thousands of years, but it's the way in which humans began to spread throughout the world.

During this time, people survived as hunters and gatherers. They migrated by sticking to the coastline. They would have caught what they could and foraged, putting the majority of their focus and time on securing food. It sounds primitive, no doubt it was. People were in a fight for survival, so work revolved around survival and food was priority number one.

Yet, what's interesting about this period in early human history is not how primitive these people were. That much you already know. The interesting thing is how humans stayed primitive for so very long. Yes, they did. When it comes to certain areas of life, things just didn't change very fast. You see, if we draw a line from today all the way back to that time – all the way back to the hunters and gatherers – in regards to work, we may see less change than you would anticipate.

Take this for instance: starting from those early humans, if we fast-forward through the next few millennia, human-kind developed a lot. We know it did. The rudiments of food production, longer-distance trade, and more extensive tools and technology were innovated. Yet, some things didn't change that much. More specifically, the overarching pursuit of work progressed at a snail's pace. As far back as we can see, the daily drive for the vast majority of people on Earth was food. It stayed that way for a very, very long time. Even during the eras of the metal ages, the Renaissance, and the Industrial Revolution, the number-one employer of all people in even the most highly developed nations was food. People worked to allow themselves and others to eat! That was the focus of our early days.

In fact, roughly until the year 1900 the majority of people in all countries were farmers. It's truly incredible. The average person born before the last hundred years, more than likely and no matter where they were from, spent their days generating food. It's what people needed to do. Even though the

Industrial Revolution, as remarkable innovations and consider-able worker specialization were occurring, food production was still the priority for the majority of people.

Yet about one hundred years ago, things changed rapidly. The need for manufacturing rose dramatically. As a result, the leading nations in the world saw an explosion in the next gener-ation of workers: blue-collar workers (people who make stuff). Their rise was so historic that by the 1950s, blue-collar workers made up about forty percent of all employment in countries like the United States. They brought with them huge change. Not only did they permanently alter the face of work, but dispos-able income, free time, and quality of life also began to shift. Massive advances were made. The fabric of entire nations was fortified and shaped. A middle class thrived. It was an unprec-edented time. But as big as the changes were, they were only just beginning. Life at the top for blue-collar workers was not to last long. They would be supplanted by a new kind of worker in a relatively short time.

Through the growth of large-scale manufacturing, the need arose for bigger and more complex organizations. Bigger orga-nizations with multiple functions – production, marketing, distribution – created the need for a new breed of employee, the white-collar worker (also known as knowledge workers). These are people who think for a living. Such employees were barely even on the map a generation earlier. But, just as dramat-ically as the earlier upswing had been for blue-collar workers, around the 1950s white-collar workers started to gain ground.

Coordinators, managers, streamliners, sales people, logistics people, and strategizers became hot commodities. How else could you produce, sell, distribute, and grow faster than your competitors? It may sound bizarre, but although many of the modern-day functions of organizations have been around for a long time, they have only just become mainstream over the past generation or two. And today, according to the U.S. Bureau of Labor Statistics, blue-collar workers make up about 5% of the national working population, farmers roughly 2%, and growing into the void these once-predominant groups have left behind, white-collar knowledge workers are standing strong.

It's only just started

On their own, these shifts in the nature of work over the past hundred years and the changes they inspired are incredible. Enough to make major waves. There is no doubt they affect the majority of the world every single day. The changes also significantly alter the choices you personally make about school, work, living situations, family, etc. For almost 200,000 years we see very little change in the pursuit of many humans' daily actions. Then, in the past hundred years we see two significant and global transformations of work, one of which you are living through. With all the changes that have occurred over the past century, it would be foolish to believe that changes in the nature of work are complete. You would be crazy to believe that. Many more changes are poised.

Now, the changes in the next phase of work may not be a move away from white-collar knowledge workers. However, the structure of organizations, the relationship between employer and employee, the duty of business... stuff like this is certainly in the mix. So are you. Whether you are seeing it now or not, you're part of this change. You're fully entrenched. Here's just a glimpse:

According to the United Nations, in 2010 the Baby Boomer generation made up thirty eight percent of the workforce, Generation X made up thirty two percent and Generation Y made up twenty five percent. By 2020, Boomers will make up less than fifteen percent, Gen X less than twenty five percent, Gen Y about fifty percent, and Gen Z about ten percent.

	Baby Boomers (Mid-1940s to mid-1960s)	Generation X (Mid-1960s to early 1980s)	Generation Y (Early 1980s to early 2000s)	Generation Z (Early 2000s to present day)
2010	38%	32%	25%	NA
2020	<15%	<25%	45-50%	10%

So, don't think for a second that there will not be drastic changes in the nature of work. This type of demographic swing will have profound effects. You can either push it forward in the best way you see fit or try to hold it back, but there is no stopping where this train is going. If you have your brakes on, reconsider your strategy.

What does all this have to do with you?

Today, computers dot every desk. Every consumer purchase involves a computer transaction. Online shopping is not just possible but necessary for many businesses. All our records are stored digitally. It can be argued that we don't need hard-copy dictionaries or thesauruses or reference material anymore. Perhaps we don't even have to know how to write or spell correctly: we have programs, apps, and wiki for all that. All we have to do is remember passwords.

Are all of these changes fundamentally good? No, but there's reason to believe they're collectively leading to a good place, albeit with growing pains.

But what does all this mean for you? Of course you know about the impact of computers: you grew up with them and you adapt to every advance with seamless ease. Damn it! Your generation is inventing the freaking technologies and software that are shaping the world. Whether technology comes easily to you or not and regardless of whether you're a techie, this stuff still comes much faster to you than to any other demographic.

It's necessary to remember that even fifteen years ago, the vast majority of workers did not even have computers on their desk. They communicated in person and by phone. They had hard copy reference material – books, articles, reports – piled in offices. They didn't have an email address (email, when it first arrived, was a serious annoyance and time-waster). Communications were typed or written by hand before being photocopied, filed, or faxed. People may have been fortunate enough to have a cell phone the size of a phone book. And maybe, if you were really cool, you had the massive thing strapped to your car.

The point is, in respect to what's possible, profitable, and even critical today for workplaces, we are only just getting our feet wet. Most organizations still have sturdy foundations in models of work that are so antiquated, they are completely foreign to any worker under the age of thirty five! Therefore, organizations and the prototypes of work still have massive change to undergo. From every angle, the workplace is still grasping to interpret the new era in which it's now immersed...

And this is what you're entering.

So don't get comfortable

In fairness, some organizations and people have started to comprehend the magnitude of these changes along with the fallout that is occurring. Perhaps this is what President Obama was referring to with his comment about the rules of work changing. Perhaps. In any event, the situation is thus: on the one side you have globalization and speed-of-light systems of supply and commerce coursing forward. On the other hand you have the traditional models of work trying to identify, understand, and keep up with developments but being over-whelmingly swallowed by the enormity of the task. Finally, in the middle you have a group of people with one foot on either side of the split, potentially getting caught in no-man's land.

You need to think differently about your career than everyone else who's come before. Traditional career advice will not be helpful because the maiden voyage in the newly emerging world of work is yours.

This evolution of work has major implications for the career paths that people have become accustomed to expect and been guided to follow. That guidance is in desperate need for an overhaul. Why? Because work is now a world that includes university dropouts building empires from their basements, and the biggest companies on the planet crafting official documents in quasi-convincing fashion in attempts to reassure stakeholders they're keeping pace when they're not. Add to this the alarming employment picture in the western world for people seeking their first career jobs and it becomes clear that the changes are happening but only a few are getting the memo.

You are now starting to get a good picture of the changes and uncertainties around work. This means that you will be forced to confront the false sense of security you may have about how you will get on in your career. This is the second in your growing list of challenges, just after the challenge of navigating from the nature of school to the nature of work. No doubt, lots is being mounted on your shoulders. The weight may be starting to feel heavy, but rest assured there are ways to alleviate the strain.

The goal: Where are we heading?

You are learning to think anew. Stage one of our journey is about reprograming your brain. As Einstein put it, "We can't solve our problems using the same thinking we used to create them." But where does this new way of thinking come from? Therein lies the problem. Most people who are in a position to offer you career advice and guidance have operated and succeeded through very different circumstances than those you face. Consequentially, much of the career direction you need to carve out for yourself must be mapped through new methods. Furthermore, the perceptions you have about work have been developed through your observations of others in an outdated model, so there's a good chance your assumptions and beliefs, once again, have to be recalibrated.

To do this, you must first accept the uncertainty around you.

Then, appreciate the journey of discovery you're on. You're not supposed to have all the answers today. Those who expect to are the ones who hit the brick wall with full force. The truth is that your answers don't yet exist, nor will they ever in perfect clarity. Finding them requires continual exploration. It is those who choose to keep looking and learning who will best find them. For now, you just need to focus your lens.

Those who are designers of their career don't think of their career as a means of work. They view it as a platform to learn about something they like; a platform to accomplish things because of what they are learning and an opportunity to share those things with others. The quest is a continual one. They're discovering how to keep from getting complacent, a characteristic that will ensure they stay on the forefront of the change they are a part of. The goal is to not be left behind.

Backtracks

Granted, this track was the macro view, not anything particularly drilled down. Yet, that doesn't make it any less impactful in your current situation or in the coming years. The evolution of work continues at a fast clip and will result in unprecedented opportunity. At the same time, it will also cause many to be caught in its wake. The problem is that no one yet knows how the changes will continue to shake out, so you simply need to stay poised and nimble.

It's the only strategy. You can't predict the outcome of the shift that is occurring. You're not even supposed to try, simply know that it is happening. Keep a watchful eye open. Then, get interested in your own journey. Understand that your career will be measured by your ability to guide it yourself. The model of work is in flux – it is the second reason the brick wall takes shape. Don't allow autopilot to kick in.

Question 5.   Given the differences in how different generations work, how do you think the coming demographic swing will impact work? (Remember, roughly sixty percent of workers will be Gen Y or Gen Z by 2020.)

Question 6.   *How have you noticed the global forces of work already affecting the lives of many workers, both positively and negatively?*

TRACK 5.
THE ENTITLEMENT
JOKE AND
DOLLO'S LAW

At a glance: Generations Y's `entitled`, `high maintenance`, `overconfident`? Give it a rest. It's time to close the useless and damaging debate.

Yeah, you're getting a bum rap. Your generation is being cast as lazy, entitled, apathetic, or worse. You're seen as different, and that difference is not well-respected in many circles. You don't fit into the professional box that has been built over the past fifty years. You're a scary uncertainty.

But don't let yourself be pulled in by the rhetoric. The world is different today: culture is different; work is different; your generation is different, and the fact that you`re different is exactly the way things are supposed to be. Different is what's needed. Different is inescapable. The evidence for these statements – or at least the supporting notion – is found in an adaptation of Dollo's Law, a longstanding theory of biological evolution (to be introduced shortly) that will give you reason to believe in what you value and why you value it. Don't believe the disparaging drivel raining down all around you. You're supposed to be different, and there's no other way it can be.

This track is about getting you to break the mould. Counter to the pressure you face, allow the work you do in your career and the way you do it to break from the norm. I urge you. The norm that many people are trying to cling to is not working out well for many.

Let's recap

You are entering the workforce at a distinctive time in history. The world is changing rapidly. This isn't news, and arguably many generations could have claimed the same. However, our world is now changing faster and in more ways than it ever has before. As we've seen in previous tracks, the changes we face are both the cause and effect of a society that is leaving production lines behind and moving at warp speed towards something new. And here's the deal; you can't afford to be left behind.

Organizations and individuals are pushing and pulling each other over boundaries, creating fundamental uncertainties about the nature of work, and the changes are only just beginning. Consequently, in your work life, failing to embrace the new way the world operates will limit your opportunities and prospects. The generation that has recently entered the workforce – you and your friends – can have unprecedented opportunity. But to convert chance to reality will require new levels of foresight, strategy, and self-control.

However, 'foresight, strategy, and self-control' have not exactly been attributes ascribed to your generation. No, your generation has many other phrases to describe them, none so polite. You're part of the entitled generation, kids who expect a lot and who are not willing to work for it. That's the popular view. But it's rubbish, also damaging. Work is poised to rise to another level. It needs to change. It can't do anything but. And you're part of the group that will make things shift. If your generation wasn't different, there would be a problem. Why this has failed to be recognized is beyond me, so don't listen to the nonsense.

Society should be helping the emerging workforce raise the bar, not lower it. You should be inspired, not demoralized. There's also reason to believe that the negative views being cast on those in your age bracket are doing little more than screwing up the launch of careers like yours. Maybe you've already fallen victim! Therefore, we recalibrate.

The usual suspects: Generation Y

This is the group of people born somewhere between the very late 1970s and the early 1990s. In sheer numbers, Gen Y is the largest generation since the Baby Boomers, who were those born in the years after the Second World War. Gen Y is now at the stage of finishing school and entering the workforce en-mass, and you may have already seen the 'high-maintenance' storyline. Here's a smattering of the headlines:

Poor verdict on Gen-Y

The jury is in on Generation Y and the verdict isn't good. Employers say Gen-Ys are short on skills, demanding, impatient, and far from loyal.

The Daily Telegraph

Hill scolds lazy gen. Y – 'They have to do their part'

Sen. Hillary Rodham Clinton lashed out at the instant-gratification generation yesterday, saying young adults "think work is a four-letter word."

New York Post

UK bosses fed up with 'graduate divas'

Daily News and Analysis

Generation Y are unmotivated slackers

A survey in October 2007 by the recruitment website CareerBuilder.com found employers complaining [Gen Y] often did not take orders well, expected to be paid more, demanded to be promoted within a year of joining and on top of all this expected to be allowed to work flexibly.

Management Issues, www.management-issues.com

Grads ambitious, demanding and overconfident

Technologically skilled, convinced they are highly employable but sometimes genuinely useless, the new British university-educated "Generation Y" is maddening employers...

Reuters

This kind of commentary has been pretty widespread. If you are already working, you've probably heard the grumblings. If you are still in school, you've most likely heard them too. The entitled label has been generously stuck to the emerging workforce.

This negative perception has become the third force that is causing the brick wall to emerge for many workers. Optimism and early career efforts are being trampled on.

Is it offensive? Annoying? Predictable? Yeah: all three.

My first boss said to me: "Tyler, people either live up, or they live down to expectations." It's one of my favourite lines, and I couldn't agree with him more. Unfortunately, not everyone has the same level of understanding. Many are still setting the stage and waiting for the emerging workforce to 'live down.' The headlines above are just the tip of the iceberg. I'm sure you will continue to come across more of these types of damaging remarks. But, shake it off. Here is how to read into this useless fodder:

The uprising

The world of work is changing beyond the comfort level for many of those who have been in the driver seats for a long time – 'the old guard'. They're seeing change happen all around them, some good, lots not. These changes have been hard to accept. Therefore, many of them wish things could go back to the way they were.

Of course, those who can read the writing on the wall and block out the noise know that this is not possible. The changes happening are real and ultimately unavoidable. Therefore, what is needed is another forward turn of the crank. The hump must be pushed past, not avoided. However, when the grip of command is being wedged from the fingers of those who've been in control, it can be a difficult understanding to accept. That is precisely why they are called the old guard.

And that's where you come in, or at least your generation. In many ways you personify the difficult changes that are occurring. Your generation embodies the uncomfortable shift the world is experiencing. And why not? You talk differently, you dress differently, you care about work in different ways. As a result you're stirring up some negative perceptions. However, the problems are not all with your generation. You just represent the change that is feared.

How it's playing out

These people – the old guard – are wondering about the ability of young people to handle the level of professionalism and competence required in the workplace. These decision-makers wonder if young employees can write and communicate well enough, if they can suspend texting habits for an entire workday, if they will know or care about the important way to conduct themselves… and more than anything else, if a generation raised on computers and choice is adequately prepared for the nature of today's work environment. On the surface, these may seem like fair concerns. You don't fit the pre-existing box. You're uncertain. And when uncertainty is rampant, things that appear uncertain don't inspire a positive response.

The old guard is very uncertain of how to fit you into their plans.

In all fairness, there is no question that today's emerging generation needs to mature in certain ways. Of course they are not perfect, nor do they make perfect choices all of the time. Fair enough. Can professionalism be improved in certain ways? Sure. Can young people become more reliable? Sure. But some of the differences young workers embody are going to be exactly what's needed to shove work, and the effect work has on our lives, in a more positive direction. I don't think anyone can argue that a shove like that is needed. Furthermore, no generation ever has been perfect. There's lots of evidence on that front (for proof, just go back and watch clips of the original Woodstock!)

This is why the belief that you need to force fit yourself into a clone of your parents or your boss is absolute garbage. Learning from them is important and valuable, but trying to create carbon copies is not. Next generations do not need to be replicas of their predecessors. Contrary thoughts are simply wrong, and more importantly they only serve to direct energy and attention away from fixing the problems our generations face together. Ideas, energy, and commitment from all of us are needed, and we end up wasting time with useless arguments.

Some people are starting to see it. In a phrase that should be printed on T-shirts and handed out en-mass, Sir Ken Robinson, one of the world's leading minds in education reform and creativity development, summed it up beautifully when he said, "We are asking the youth of today to fill our shoes; what is so good about our shoes?" Exactly.

Enter Dollo's Law

So curl your fingers into a ball and leave one sticking up, any finger you want, to those who say your generation is broken, hopeless, or poised to do the world wrong. It's just not true. That's why the point of this track is to provide new perspective on the Gen Y difference, aimed at giving you a way to understand and value the way you approach work. The new perspective comes from a reconsideration of Dollo's Law of Irreversibility, with a slight twist. It's a law used to describe the way in which living things change, a theory in biological evolution. It also flies in the face of the typical generational banter and provides some much-needed clarity.

So, who is Dollo and what's his law? Well, Louis Antoine Marie Joseph Dollo (1857 – 1931) was a French vertebrate paleontologist. Before gaining recognition in paleontology, Dollo was trained and worked as an engineer. A rare combination of skills indeed, but perhaps the perfect combination of knowledge and deductive ability to lead him to contribute new ideas on the theory of evolution. After field work unearthing dinosaur bones and fossils in Belgium, Dollo recognized factors that led him to propose the following theory:

> An organism is unable to return, even partially, to a previous stage already realized in the ranks of its ancestors.

This statement is known as Dollo's Law of Irreversibility, and it means that an organism never returns exactly to its former state and complex structures. It means that features and characteristics, once lost, are not regained in their original form. Put another way, once evolution occurs, we cannot turn back the clock.

It is a strikingly uncomplicated proposition, one that casts the evolution of all systems in a whole new light. The natural phenomenon of evolution is a process that happens at its own pace and under the control of environment and chance. It shapes all life, and not just through DNA changes. All living systems evolve... whether plants, societies, or generations. Each of these complex entities is in continual flux. And once change happens, it can never go back. It is the moulding force of populations. That's why it's fair to say:

> *A generation is unable to return, even partially, to a previous stage already realized in the ranks of its ancestors.*

Just like organisms must bend, shift, and ultimately mutate to handle the current state of affairs in their environments, so too must the generations we belong to. This is done through forward progress, not by retracing steps. That's what Generation Y has done. They've grown up by bending and shifting with the current state of affairs. You've simply become a generation that reflects the nature of your times.

What Dollo's Law means to you now

Dollo's Law is a beautifully simple theory which allows you to be unapologetic about who you are, what you care about, and what you want to do with your life. It's rooted in the evolutionary theory that continues to guide science, and it should become a belief adopted by emerging generations as they fight to break the irrational cycle of older generations telling younger generations they need to start looking and acting more like them. For me, Dollo's Law has been a 'paradigm shifter' of sufficient force to shatter some ill-conceived notions I had when starting my career. It has also been a powerful tool that guided me to reconsider doing things simply because they had 'always been done that way'. I believe it will have the same beneficial effect for you.

In plain language, Dollo's Law gives you the moral fortitude to stand strong when people complain that the emerging generation is too unprofessional, too spoiled, or too entitled. For the wave of people who are just starting to hit the shores of a world of work that is calling for unprecedented levels of innovation, this notion could not come at a better time. New problems require new solutions, and in order to ignite ideas and innovation, a changed outlook is required. To that end, the concept behind Dollo's Law is not just an academic discussion or an intergenerational spitting war.

For these reasons, Dollo's Law is a message worth spreading. You see, it is necessary for all of us to get it through our collectively thick skull that the generation currently entering the workforce is not screwed up. They are not leading the world to certain doom. They will carry the social and economic torches just fine. You can tell those who would say differently to go (fill in the blank). This chapter gives you anthropological and evolutionary evidence to do just that.

Putting the argument to rest

Dollo's Law also infers that for societies – indeed, for humanity – to collectively confront and solve today's challenges, we must look for new solutions. It will not be enough to run through the inventory of old answers. The sooner we figure this out, the faster we can all get to solving problems that truly matter rather than wasting energy on repetitive, unconstructive, and meaningless debate about the 'deficiencies' of new generations. The sooner we figure this out, the faster we can stop the career merry-go-round that has people blindly jumping on board, starting work, hoping to find a fulfilling career, following the same footsteps as everyone else, and then being surprised when their careers end up in the same disappointing place.

Remember, beyond a shadow of a doubt, the generations that have come before us have improved life, culture, and work. To not acknowledge this is gravely disrespectful and stifling to the immense amount of learning that has gone on before you. There are lots of lessons to learn from those who have explored before you. But on the flip side, previous generations have not perfected civilization. Collectively, we still have a lot of room for growth. Work is evolving and society is evolving. The goal is to find synchronicity.

With Dollo's Law in mind, I suggest you shift your view of work beyond the boundaries you currently see. Maybe not overnight, but with unbiased thought, yes. There are good examples of people and organizations who are doing exactly this. If you look at the style and nature of work in some of the most progressive companies, you'll see they've already started the shift. Why? Well, for lots of reasons, but one of them is because they realize the name of the game in today's world is innovation. You see, when outdated traditions of work are allowed to be broken, the power of invention takes over. And while it is productive to explore innovative ways of doing things at any time, the need increases exponentially during times of large-scale change... and we are certainly facing a time of large-scale change. So, feel confident about the things that excite you in life and in work. Whole new industries, jobs, and ways of working are on the horizon. Many of them have started already. You will learn how to seek out these possibilities.

But first, there's something else on the menu. Before you get ahead of yourself, before you get too self-assured, it is time to eat your slice of humble pie. Because, while Dollo's Law has given you reason to be confident; the following track offers the counterpunch.

Backtracks

You should be able to start filling in the blanks. I have not been overly obvious with the storyline in this book because it is important to think for yourself. The three forces you have been reading about relate back to the formation of the brick wall. As you know, young workers often hit that wall with full force, so it makes sense to know the reasons why it arises. There are still a few more reasons to follow, but at this point you know that the brick wall is hit because the systems of work and school differ so drastically. Also, because the world of work is evolving so quickly, people are having trouble keeping pace with what that means. And finally, because young workers are confronting a workplace where many believe they are destined to fail.

If you want to minimize the effect the brick wall will have on you, don't get pulled in by the generational banter.

Question 7.   *How do you think a poor perception of your generation is affecting people at work?*

Question 8.   *Knowing that generations are supposed to look and be different, how can you show new confidence in your approach to work?*

TRACK 6.
YOUR PIECE OF HUMBLE PIE: THE CHOICE DEFECT

At a glance: There is good reason to believe in yourself, your identity and your unique way forward. First, however, recognize how the Choice Defect may be leading you astray.

The message of this track is best introduced through a story. The following is a personal anecdote, but there are many others that could fit the bill. As particular as this situation seems, the circumstances it describes are anything but unique.

***

"Seriously, how much do you think one of those things weighs?" I turned to my Dad to ask for roughly the tenth time that day. "They look really freaking heavy!"

In response, all I got back was a tired, sweaty glare and the few words, "For the last time, just try to ask." So, using what little Mandarin I knew at the time, I finally did.

Here's the setting. You've probably seen it in postcards. Huangshan, or Yellow Mountain, is the famous craggily peaked mountain you often see in Chinese photos. It's the one with trees that look like the Bonsais in The Karate Kid, and finger-like peaks that emerge from a sea of mist as they rise towards the sky. It's worth Googling. My Dad and I had been on an overnight train to get there, and after a short sleep bunking with a family who taught us how to play Mahjong and served us fried rice, we were en-route to the top of this peak. As treacherous as the mountain appears, the hike is really not as problematic as you would imagine. As a UNESCO heritage site, Huangshan has exchanged narrow paths and steep scrambles for a never-ending string of stairs carved into the side of the mountain. A shame, but fair enough. What the mountain gave up in sketchy walkways that forced you to take your life in your hands, it's gained in quad-burning agony as you climb over 4000 steps stretching 1000 vertical metres.

The two of us had been climbing for hours through some of the most beautiful surroundings I have ever experienced. Yet, something else during this breathtaking journey continued to capture our attention. Now please understand, we're talking about one of the most scenic spots on Earth. So spectacular, in fact, that it was part of the inspiration for James Cameron's Avatar. Therefore, anything that pulls your attention certainly has a reason for standing out. The thing we could simply not take our eyes off was the long string of men we were slowly climbing past: men carrying huge loads of supplies strung to bamboo sticks resting on their shoulders.

In order to appreciate it, try your best to picture this. Take a three- to four-foot length of bamboo about three inches in diameter. Slice it vertically from top to bottom, leaving a long half-moon shaped stick. Then, tie loads of water, concrete mix, or whatever you want to each side of the stick with a three-foot length rope. Finally, put the stick on your shoulders, curved part down, and start walking. This is the image of the men we continued to walk around as we climbed more than 4000 stairs.

Within first glance of these guys, it's impossible not to notice the volume of stuff they carry. It's an enormous amount of supplies they huff up to the two hotels at the top of the mountain. So, it's these bamboo sticks on shoulders with piles of swinging supplies tied to the end of ropes I am referencing in the question I continue to pester my Dad with. And, as mentioned, I did finally fumble my way through the words to ask one of the men how heavy their loads were.

"How much weigh?" I asked. His response made me question the little bit of Mandarin I knew.

"Sixty to seventy kilos," the man said.

"Sixty kilos?" I ask back.

"Yes, sixty kilos," he affirms.

In my head, I'm thinking 'No way!' but being the guy who needs to learn the hard way, I ask, "Can I try?" In return, he looks at me with a questioning stare, almost like he's sizing me up, and motions me over to the bamboo stick. I too size up the guy (who couldn't have weighed more than 140 pounds soaking wet), walk over with confidence and grab the stick.

Over the past dozen years of my life, it is fair to say that I have spent enough time in a gym to be familiar with how much certain things weigh. Anyone who does a little strength training knows that 135 pounds is a common weight. It's the weight of a standard Olympic bar with a forty-five pound plate on each side. In kilograms, it's 61 kg. With these calculations in mind as I grabbed the bamboo bar, I had little doubt I would be able to confirm if this load was sixty to seventy kilos. As I ducked my head under the bar and slowly raised the loads off the ground, I clearly remember thinking, 'This guy's not lying. This damn thing weighs 135 pounds.' That was my first thought. My second thought came after I tried to climb three or four stairs carrying the load and almost dropped to my knees because I couldn't control the weight swinging at the end of the ropes. No way do these guys carry their body weight in supplies, swinging on rope, 4000 steps up the side of a mountain! I couldn't even carry it three steps.

You see, these men carry these supplies because it's their job. Is it agony? I have to assume so, yes. But, they're making a living. And in rural China in 2007, these men didn't have a lot of other options. They could either migrate to the big city to expand their employment options, or they could choose a job like this and climb. It's the type of decision people are faced with when they're not born in a place where opportunities are abundant. Millions of people face this decision. Millions more don't even have that choice; they can't get to a place where their employment options improve. Unlike in China, a blossoming city is not on their horizon. It is a sad reality.

Thankfully, in many places world-wide this type of situation is turning around for countless people. In countries where only a generation ago very little existed in terms of life options, major strides forward are now being taken. They're striving to get to a place where their people have opportunity. They're trying to get to a place where their people have choice. It is one of the fundamental pursuits in society, and it's a powerful force.

Please keep this in mind as you read the rest of this track.

Choice and a game-changing perspective

Almost a decade ago I'd started my observations of the school-to-work predicament, but I had yet to understand what I was seeing. No doubt I was well-versed in the symptoms of the transitional problem I knew existed. However, I had no idea of the root cause. The symptoms were typical: young graduates jumping between jobs, travelling to break from a role they knew was not for them, or slowly sliding to settle into a dejected state of duty. Predictable they became. Yet what was causing these symptoms was much more difficult to identify.

I was searching for the foundational concept that would allow the pattern to neatly fall into place. I knew the problem existed. I knew what it looked like. I even knew what it was causing. But why? Why was it occurring? Why were so many people falling into this trap? For the longest time, I didn't know. It wasn't until I came across a certain thought laden statement tucked away in an article that the puzzle pieces started to come together to form a picture that made sense. It filled in the blanks and quickly became my new centre of gravity for the slice of the working world I was studying. I finally had the concept from which everything else could stem. For the first time, I begun to understood the fundamental cause of why so many young people struggle with their entrance into work. So what was that statement?

Well, before you read it, a brief introduction is needed

When he died at 95, he was still the man. Peter Drucker, that is. If you aren't familiar with his work, a little reading is worth your time. He's the father of management and organizational study and arguably the best forecaster of societal change the world's seen in a hundred years. Thus, his words carry some weight. So, I suggest you read the next bit with full attention.

Over to Mr. Drucker; this is the statement that changed my career and life:

> *In a few hundred years, when the history of our time is written from a long-term perspective, it is likely that the most impor-*
> *tant event those historians will see is not technology, not the*
> *Internet, not e-commerce. It is an unprecedented change in*

the human condition. For the first time – literally – substan-
tial and rapidly growing numbers of people have choices. For
the first time, they will have to manage themselves. And
society is totally unprepared for it. (Peter Drucker, 2001)

If you want to know why your generation is different, you just read it. You may have thought what set you apart is computers, the Internet, or some other grand advancement in technology, but you'd be wrong. The difference is choice.

Even before you enter your career, the choices you face are abundant. Where to go to school? Should you go to school? What field? What city? Should you take on a student loan? What will you do for work when you graduate? You face an overload of choices. In comparison to the generations that have come before you, and through the lens of history, this is anything but normal. The level of choice you face is new.

Obviously, choice has been around for much longer than you've been alive, you might offer. Of course it has, but not to this degree. Never to this degree. The generation currently coming into the workforce, your generation, is being exposed to and raised with choice like never before; choice that arrived whether they realized it or not and choice that requires people to grasp a new level of self-management. As Drucker states, "society is totally unprepared for it."

It's interesting: when most people think about the information age, they think technology. But what they fail to recognize is that technology has simply been the vehicle. The true effect of the information age is the impact technology and information are having on the lives of people they touch. It's not technology that's changing lives, it's choice. That's why the information age is a lifestyle movement as much as it is anything else. Drucker understood this and described the phenomenon as "… an unprecedented change in the human condition. For the first time – literally – substantial and rapidly growing numbers of people have choices." And so it is: the biggest change we see in today's world is the rise of choice. If you don't believe me, go visit a country that has many of their people experiencing choice for the first time, like China. That will be all the convincing you need.

Double-edged sword

Choice and the evolution of work are complementary developments. They fit hand-in-hand. Civilization has been working for over 200,000 years to get the opportunities of work and life to the point they are. It's truly amazing. Yet, in a twist that cannot be considered anything but ironic, although opportunity has been a pursuit of people for as long as we have been around, the very thing we've been striving for, choice, is causing new levels of problems in our world. As great as choice is, and as much as we fight to never have it taken away, it is proving to be a double-edged sword.

Choice is creating new types of issues, issues society didn't see coming. These are issues that stem from, as Drucker insinuates, the inability to effectively manage ourselves. There are many current examples. Stuff like the obesity epidemic and the poor state of financial management are but two of the obvious examples that stem from an abundance of choice. But, real-life examples don't stop there. The impact of choice quickly expands beyond the obvious and certainly finds an important place in this discussion of careers. Choice is the specific reason why the notion of Career Design is coming to a head now, during your career era. Choice in the world of work is abundant for the first time in history. For this reason, as much as your career will be about learning, thinking and doing, it will be just as much about effectively dealing with choice. It will be about self-management.

Unprecedented choice is causing many of the career challenges you face. Therefore, your ability to deal with the choices you face will be a determining factor in your journey at work. It will be your ability to self-manage that will allow you to take hold of the immense opportunities that dot the horizon of your career. Unfortunately, the opposite is equally true. And right now, when it comes to dealing with choice, your generation is not starting strong.

Self-management and your piece of humble pie

Even though it's Drucker, we would be remiss to take his words at face value on reputation alone. We must ask ourselves: is choice really having the impact he believed it would? And if so, why? Can it be that "society is totally unprepared for it?" These are questions that must be asked, so let's break it down.

First, although we commonly use the word 'choice' to describe the circumstances facing a growing number of people in today's world, it's not really choice that's the issue. It's the fact that choice requires a decision. The decision point and the aftermath which ensues are where complications arise. Choice is just the nicely packaged word becoming popularized to describe a pretty complex phenomenon. We have grown to appreciate the value of choice, but not decisions. And since choice needs a decision, it's a problem. It's your problem. Although you are a generation of choice, you are also a generation of terrible decision-makers. Failure to own up to this fact is a weighty error. In fact, making decisions is your biggest collective generational flaw.

Generation Y doesn't have an entitlement problem. Rather, they have a decision-making problem. Is one issue any better than the other? Not necessarily, but the solutions to fix the two problems differ. Consequentially, we need to fix your inability to make decisions, not your sense of entitlement. You suck with decisions. This is your piece of humble pie, and it's a prerequisite to eat before moving forward in your career and life. Choice is the fourth force which causes the brick wall to appear in your journey.

Yet, there is hope. At least the challenge has been identified. You know where to start your recovery. Everything else you have read up until now has been about the forces that surround you, pushing and pulling on your career. These are forces that are beyond your control. All you can do is recognize and work with them. But this one – choice: this force is one you can deal

with on your own. Finally, you have your first grip of control.
Now you have some leverage. Thankfully, it doesn't need to be a
damper. If you can learn to be a better decision-maker, if you can
learn to better manage yourself, life is yours to grab by the horns.

The Choice Effect

Choice is so ingrained in our culture that we often forget to
appreciate the potential it carries. Generations ago, the magnitude of choice experienced today was beyond imagine. Think
back only one hundred years to our farming ancestors. Life
was extremely different on so many fronts. Today, we make
hundreds of small decisions every day about the coffee we
want to drink or the shirt we want to buy, but we also make
major decisions too. We make decisions on choices that were
not available to people before like education, home life, and
career. These choices, some believe, have become a blinding
force for this generation. A couple of lights to guide the way
are a great thing, but too much light is just the opposite: it's
blinding. Choice can work in the same sort of way. It can
become a sincerely overwhelming presence.

Although choice is a crowning achievement of human rights,
it is also proving to be the kryptonite in many areas of our lives.
The blinding force of choice has a name. It is described as the
Choice Effect, coined in a book by Amalia McGibbon, Lara
Vogel, and Claire Williams. Those authors specifically char-
acterize the phrase in this way: "The twenty- and thirty some-
things who have all the opportunity in the world and no clue
how to decide between them."

The Choice Effect spawned off Barry Schwartz's work, the
Paradox of Choice, and the concept has proven very useful.
The struggle the Choice Effect describes is establishing itself as
a mighty foe. However, the effect is only one side of the choice
coin, and perhaps the pretty side at that. The other side of the
coin shows a much more sinister face.

Choice's ugly twin: The Choice Defect

If the front side of the choice issue is the Choice Effect, the backside is something I call the Choice Defect. It's Choice Effect's ugly twin, and it's become a very troubling mindset that seems to have infiltrated your generation. As much as you struggle with choosing between several options, you probably struggle even more with sticking to the decisions you've already made.

The Choice Defect is best described as the belief that a back door escape hatch exists out of any situation one faces. It's the ejector seat people believe they can use to get themselves out of discomfort. More precisely, it's the notion that is psychologically evolving into us that leads us to think that because we've always had opportunity and always had choice, a better option is readily available and it's only one small move away.

The Choice Defect is the reason we second guess our decisions. It's the reason we have trouble getting over the uncomfortable hump that must be overcome in order to get to the place in life we're shooting for. The Choice Defect is that little bird on your shoulder telling you to turn and try something else when you've only just started option one. We see others who produce results faster or achieve more, and we think we've only to change what we do so that we can do that too. So, we abandon the path we're on in an attempt to follow. And then, sooner than later we realize we've wound up stuck between all our options because we had trouble pursuing any one path long enough. That's the Choice Defect. It's also a spawn of the Paradox of Choice, and as you might imagine, it's one hell of a powerful force. I should know: I felt it strongly during the early stages of my career. Who knows? The writing of this book may be a direct result.

Getting caught up in the magnetic pull of the Choice Defect to a certain degree is a reality for all of us who were fortunate enough to be born into a situation of choice. And of course, its allure is not necessarily bad by rule. Evaluating your decisions is a part of learning: a big part. That's what exploring is all about. If the path you chose to swap your current one for is truly the better path, second-guessing yourself was a good thing. But, and it's a big but, if the path you were on was leading to a good place and all that was required was a little focus, hard work, and perseverance to get over the hump, the escape hatch you took early ends up being a terrible choice.

Where the Choice Defect is leading you

Choice is great, but not if it causes you to constantly look over your shoulder at what you gave up. Careers become very problematic if you are quick to make decisions and take on new paths in life before a fair evaluation of your current situation has occurred. By doing that, perhaps you're just jumping from one proverbial frying pan into another. Or potentially, you're giving up on a situation that had the opportunity to deliver exactly what you were looking for all along. The reality is, you see, that you are potentially facing a situation where none of the options you have at the current time is a perfect fit, but given a little time, one or more may become so. Coming to grips with this is one of the hardest things for young people.

In one of the response letters I received from a CEO (remember I wrote to all those Fortune 500 CEO's during my early career panic), I was advised that young employees who discover the most success find an appropriate balance between patience and urgency. It was very well-articulated advice. Unfortunately, however, most don't find that balance early enough. As a result, they find themselves jumping from situation to situation or job to job, playing career hopscotch and ending up lost. It's the perfect Catch-22. People never put in enough effort to break beyond the initial challenge they face; they forgo putting in enough effort because they are quick to believe work is not designed to offer what they want. Many get caught in that spiraling trap, stuck between effort and picking a new option. Others, however, learn to avoid the trap altogether. And it's that slight deviation, that small difference in how we deal with choice, which becomes one of the biggest separators in the trajectory of a career.

For many, when it comes to their careers, it's not the number of choices they face that delivers the biggest blow. It's not the Choice Effect. It's the tension that begins to build after the first decision has already been made. It's the Choice Defect. Consequentially, it's not the front side of choice that will toss and turn you into a miserable state; it's the backside.

On the surface it looks like you are ducking out of the challenge because you don't like to work hard or because you feel entitled. To the contrary, what may be occurring is that you want to find your calling, work hard, achieve, serve, earn, and produce so badly that you are frantically searching for the best place to do those things. And when something doesn't show immediate promise, you pull the rip cord. The tragedy, though, is that you just didn't know how to put your best intentions to use, and nobody offered this tiny piece of guidance. Consequently, instead of finding your footing you become a victim of the Choice Defect and easily get lead astray.

Backtracks

You were born with the gift of choice, moreso than almost anyone who has come before your time. You aren't faced with carrying sixty kilos up the side of a mountain to earn a living. You rarely need to leave your family and way of life to seek out employment elsewhere. You have been afforded the opportunity of choice; don't let it go to waste. Worse yet, don't let it be the very thing that takes you down.

If Dollo's Law has given you reason for going after new things, believing in yourself, and carving a unique path forward, the Choice Defect should be the sobering wake-up call. On one hand you should feel empowered and re-energized. On the other, you should be acutely aware of how you have allowed yourself to quickly be pulled in new directions. Smarten up.

Your generation is terrible at making decisions. In part, this is because the number of choices you face can be blinding. However, most people find a way to deal with the volume of options they face. The bigger issue with choice arises for people when they have already made a decision and now feel an overpowering urge to go try something new. They choose option A and then quickly jump ship to option B because it suddenly appears to be the better choice. This is the Choice Defect. It is one of the biggest reasons why the brick wall is hit, and subsequently why careers begin to split down two diverging paths.

What many fail to realize is that there is a good chance that neither option A nor option B is the perfect fit: they may only become so after you work to get over the hump, work to make that option fit, and work to stay focused. So, please beware of the Choice Defect.

Question 9. *Think about the scenarios you read every day in the news. Was Peter Drucker right? Is the world unprepared for people to manage themselves?*

Question 10. *Think back in your own life: What is the scenario that immediately comes to mind when you think about the difficulties you have had managing choice?*

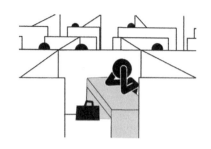

TRACK 7.
YOU'RE KIDDING ME: THE REALITY OF ENTRY LEVEL WORK

At a Glance: Entry level work is tough, frustrating and infuriating. It has a subtle way of surprising you. Prepare for the real career shake-up that occurs.

Full disclosure: In a later track I describe and fully defend the Career Design mentality that work doesn't need to suck or even be a burden. It's a notion that may be counter to your current beliefs or situation. I argue that work is one of the best platforms in life to contribute to and make an individual mark on the world. I provide strong reasoning as to why work no longer needs to be about work per se, rather that it can be about learning, exploring, discussing, showing, teaching, practicing – the types of things we find enjoyable outside of work. However, given all that, given my unshakeable belief that modern-day work and the way you go about it can break the old mentality that work is only about the daily toil... entry level work deserves an asterisk. It's a slight exception. Work doesn't need to suck, but entry level work sucks. That is, unless you can turn it in your favour.

Yeah, it's a contradictory message. Work can and should be this great thing, but your first job or two, well, that's different. Entry level jobs, they're just a different animal, not designed to be wonderful. It's contradictory, and contradictory it will remain. Entry level work is a difficult moment in people's careers. Not difficult because the work is so challenging, but difficult because the work is often quite easy, even mundane, and the role doesn't offer the things you believed you would be earning by entering your career – more freedom and control.

As a result, as much as the transition from one system to another, the evolution of work, Dollo's Law, and the Choice Defect are mighty forces that help raise the brick wall in your career, the reality of entry level work may be the mightiest force of all. It makes just as many people stumble as the other forces. Even if you can find a way to traverse the other major issues that dot the early career minefield, the potentially deflating reality of entry level work is the final deadly tripwire.

Entry level work is tough, but it's tough for all. You must get through it.

Light at the end

In a sense, entry level work is a rite of passage. In order to fully step into the career you envision, you must pass through this broad band of employment first. Is it a fun passage? It could be worse, I can say that much. As a rite of passage to become a warrior, the Satere-Mawe tribe in the Brazilian Amazon requires would-be warriors to put their hands in gloves lined with bullet ants, one of the world's most painful insect stingers, for ten minutes – pure agony. Entry level work's not that bad, but it is still a rite of passage like any rite of passage. Of course, by getting through you don't enter the warrior brotherhood or some secret society; it's nothing like that. But, you do enter a domain of work that's much more appealing. You enter a domain that allows you to start earning the types of things you believe to be the pursuit of your career. Yet to get there, you first need to remain intact through the entry level trials and tribulations.

As you now know, entry level work is the period when many careers split towards either dejection or success. The split is what happens after the brick wall is hit. You may even be at those crossroads now. If you are, I ask you to assert that entry level work will not be the reason why you drift away from the path of promise.

I say this because as frustrating as entry level work may seem, rest assured that most early career jobs are the same. So what you're in for, everyone else is in for too. Laughably few days off? You bet. Days of frenzy followed by days of boredom? Of course. Work you do that goes nowhere? For sure. I know that I was forced to take a deep breath to suppress my frustration. That's why there's good reason to be cautious before bouncing between jobs and looking for something better: lots of these roles are the same. No job may be able to offer what you're looking for yet.

So give it a little time: if you can just get over the hump, who knows? Maybe the job you have now can offer the prospects you're looking for. Your perspective can change. That's why the entry level game is as much patience as it is strategy. That's the quick advice for those who are currently in these throes and may be floundering. For those who have yet to get there, the simple knowledge of what to expect may be all the preparation you need.

Entry level work

We'll start by discussing why it is the way it is. Remember, it was after tasting my first few jobs that I said to myself, 'I went to school that long for this?' I wasn't alone in my sentiments. My early career observations, mixed with countless discussions with entry level workers, have been overtly clear. Entry level work surprises many people. Therefore, there must be a reason it conjures this type of reaction. Honestly! Why is entry level work the way it is?

It's a simple explanation. Organizations need someone to do their front-line work. They need someone to interact with their customers, answer the phones, carry out the decisions of others, and basically do the grunt work. So, they allocate their entry level employees. Who else would they choose? It makes sense. The difficulty is that type of work - the grunt work - is certainly not the type of work you were hoping to encounter in your career. It's also not the type of work you have been training for in school. At school you're doing assignments like you're the CEO. But this... this is extremely tedious work (a few other adjectives could be used to describe it too). Yet, it's work that must be done.

In many ways, the organizational decision to have entry level people do the front-line work is very rational, but that doesn't mean there isn't room for improvement. Lots could be done to better engage the emerging workforce. Some organizations are already doing this. It's to their advantage. The more people you can stop from going down the dejected work path, the greater collective effort the organization gains back in return.

Unfortunately though, most organizations haven't figured out how to do this yet. Regardless, at this stage of your game, as an entry level employee, improvement of the system is not what should be on your mind. There's time for that later. For now, simply getting through the passage is paramount.

It's also necessary to reinforce that, in an uncanny way, entry level jobs look excessively alike all across the world of work. Of course, specific duties from job to job may alter, and professions and trades tend to have a big leg up due to their specializations, but the nature of entry level work has an eerie set of common characteristics that paint most jobs with the same brush. That's why entry level work includes a lot of crap, regardless of the job you have.

Consequentially, if you find yourself cursing your current job, remember that it may not be the job that's terrible, just the stage of work. With that in mind, the goal is to focus on the things in your early career that you can control and the rest, well, just let slip away. Entry level jobs have been inbred for years to look and feel as similar as possible. To an extent, the model's broken, yes, but it's the reality you must learn to navigate.

Together in battle

Take solace in the following: the transition from school to work is one of the most upheaving life changes you will ever go through. Further, the upheaval is not unique to you; everyone feels it. And in terms of major life shakeups, my guess is that having children probably tops that list, but right below would be stuff like career entry, marriage, divorce, and retirement. So expect it. No matter what job you get, the start of your career will radically alter your lifestyle, expectations, financial earnings, spending habits, holidays, friendships, weight... the list goes on and on. The trouble is, most of those factors don't alter for the better.

Many of the elements that create lifestyle changes through entry level work are somewhat predictable, and most others are easy to identify once you've been through the transition and have enough time and space to look back. That's why most of the older people you meet give you the impression they're career experts. However, take their expertise with a grain of salt. As we've discussed, the world has changed, not in all ways, but in many. The expertise of those who made their way in the world of work a few decades ago is time-limited. You know the rules have changed. That's why for those who are still in the entry level storm, the challenge faced is significant. Your venture into work will drastically shake up your life. Plus, work's different. Don't underestimate the challenge. Your entry into work is not just a paycheque thing; it's a life thing.

In this light, you begin to taste the reality of entry level work. It can be a tough pill to swallow. You see, for many people, work makes you realize that you may never again have a life-style with as much free time or carefree enjoyment as you did when you were in school. I can think of more enjoyable conclusions to be faced with in life than that. But, your reluctance to accept that fact doesn't change its accuracy. Career work brings with it a different stage of life. You must come to grips with it.

Entry level work and the lifestyle shakeup

School is a blessed stage of life. You may not feel that way while you're in it, but don't kid yourself: school's great. Work's different. Work brings with it a different stage of life. That's not to say that life stops being fun once you graduate! The fun just shifts; there are a few more strings attached. That's why starting work needs to be looked at from a lifestyle perspective.

Work significantly alters your routine and your freedom. This may seem obtusely obvious. We all know work will shake up how we spend our time. We also know it will force us to alter the way we go about doing what we do during the productive hours of our week. But, because this lifestyle change seems so obvious, we don't give the impact of this shakeup a second thought. That's where our mistake is made.

What we fail to recognize is that the broad strokes that painted almost all entry level jobs to look the same also gave them a few common characteristics that affect the lifestyle of young workers in very similar ways. And on top of the fact that entry level work asks you to do the mundane chores of an organization, which is not fun in its own right, the lifestyle change it requires you to undergo can also be a rude awakening. Entry level work is full of little wrinkles, and time and freedom are but two.

So how exactly does entry level work alter your lifestyle? Let's talk day-to-day routine.

Work = Time

Your entry level job will provide you with less free time than you had in school. That's almost a universal law of nature. Exceptions include student athletes, heavily involved students, those who work full-time jobs on top of school, and liars. But, aside from those exceptions, the transition from school to work will require your actual hours of dedicated work to expand. In simple language, this means you'll put in more hours a week at work than you did at school.

Of course, there is variance depending on the country you work in. According to the Organization for Economic Cooperation and Development (OECD), the number of hours worked varies by nation. In 2012, the countries on the higher side were Mexico and South Korea at 2,226 and 2,090 annual hours worked (divided over 50 weeks this is 44.5 and 41.8 hours of work per week). On the low side are the Netherlands and Germany at 1,381 and 1,397 annual hours apiece (27.6 and 27.9 hours per week). The United States comes somewhere in the middle at 1,790 per year (or 35.8 hours per week), so too does Canada at 1,710 (or 34.2 hours per week).

Now, these may seem slightly lower than you expect, but don't be fooled. These are average work weeks, which means it includes all workers from restaurant servers, to bankers, to plumbers. It also strips away every minute of "unpaid" time like lunch and coffee breaks, so take the numbers for what they are. The average career job in most developed countries is going to push forty hours a week at the least.

School, on the other hand, does not take up forty hours a week. Not of true working time, at least. But, take one step outside of school into your entry level job and your day-to-day routine alters in an instant. The hours of work per week take a significant jump. This is especially true if you work for an organization whose culture calls for many more hours per week than forty, and many do. As a result, work will undoubtedly change your schedule for the worse. This is one part of the life-style change that comes with entry level work.

Over and over again

The greater consequence to the early career lifestyle transition is not so much a matter of time, but of consistency. For those who just left school, you should be well-acquainted with this notion. If you skip class once in a while or decide that today is the day to sleep in, nobody notices or cares. But they do at work. Entry level jobs, in fact all jobs, don't afford the luxury of inconsistency. Again, this is something you know but have yet to internalize. For many people entering their career, the newly required consistency of scheduling is not one that develops immediately. It takes a while for the new schedule to normalize. Not because these people are lazy or irresponsible. Rather, they're just caught off-guard. Work requires a mental shift, and there's some lag time in the adjustment. Sadly, organizations aren't patient. As soon as you're hired they expect the professional behaviours they demand. No leeway. So, when we think back to the Leadership IQ study, the one that said forty six percent of newly hired employees fail within the first eighteen months, inconsistency would have been the type of behaviour breakdown the study would have been talking about.

Being on time and being there all of the time matter a lot.

Not just for a week or a quarter, but for the long haul. Even on those days when it's an absolute grind to haul your butt out of bed and get yourself into work on time, you must with consistency. Now that you're employed, not only do you need to work longer hours, but the consistency of those hours needs to improve as well. This is the reality of entry level work and it's thrown on top of your daily duties (the ones you may or may not even care for). That's how it all begins: you quickly realize you're consistently adhering to a routine and a longer schedule for a job you don't even like. It's easy to see how doubt creeps in. Hence, the brick wall.

How much vacation time?

Unfortunately, I'm not done with the bad news. The changes to your lifestyle are not just a factor of daily time and routine, they're also about your freedom. Freedom in your career is something we're going to touch on in more depth in a later track, but for the time being let's only look at career freedom from the vacation perspective. Work will offer much less vacation time than you have ever experienced before (a few exceptions exist). For me, this was the most difficult part of my young career to accept. Vacation time at the start of your career is abhorrent. At least in most countries it is. My first real job, the one with the Edmonton Oilers, received two weeks of vacation a year. That's not fourteen days, but ten. In North America this is standard for entry level work. Other countries fare better. Australians, for instance, start with at least twenty days of paid vacation a year. Either way, this is a far cry from the days off and flexibility you had while in school. Yes, I know what you are thinking. Many students work summer jobs while in school. But, the majority still tend to have greater flexibility than their 'career' working peers. This is especially true when you factor in the winter holidays and reading week (spring break).

Early in your career, your expectation should be to have as little as ten days off a year plus national holidays. That's ten days off a year to plan vacations, road trips, family get-togethers, and down time. The transition from school to work requires a drastic change in your routine, consistency, and vacations. Travellers be forewarned! The outlook is grim.

Enough is enough

This is a good place to stop. We could take this track further, talk more and more of the other early career wrinkles you'll discover, but for the time being this is enough. We've covered the big stuff. No need to overwhelm. Also, let me remind you: this track is not designed to get you feeling more jaded than you may already be. It is merely trying to communicate the true reality of entry level work: the stuff that lies just below the surface. If you let it sink in, you'll appreciate the implications of what you have just read.

Please keep in mind that there are strategies to guide you through and even speed up this transition; they're coming later. Furthermore, the Career Design movement is figuring out ways to start building the lifestyle factors back into work (the ones you lose early in your career that are worth earning back). So don't stop reading here! Entry level work isn't all bad, it's just the start of a long journey. Like I said, it's a rite of passage.

I reinforce this message for a very specific reason. If you're currently in the entry level stage of your career, better days are on the horizon... but you must get there yourself. Nothing comes automatically anymore. The ocean is big. You must swim and keep swimming. The entry level stage of work is a critical period, and you can't allow yourself to lose steam. Many do.

Backtracks

Entry level work sucks. So be it. It does lead to a better place. Furthermore, everyone experiences it: almost all jobs look the same and there is no way out but through. Therefore, dig in and get over the hump. That's the big take-away from this track.

However, it's also important to know why entry level jobs suck. Aside from the daily tasks they require you to do that are often quite boring and mundane, entry level work will require you to work more hours than you ever have in the past. It will require you to be more consistent. And to top it off, it will offer fewer days off for vacation than you may have expected. Yes, there is good reason why people don't fall in love with their first job. But you can't let these factors mount and push you onto the dejected path. You have been warned what to expect. You are now starting to get a picture of the true challenge of the early stages of career work.

Question 11. *In what ways did entry level work surprise you? If you are not yet there, how do you anticipate it surprising you?*

Question 12. *How will you protect against the small, hidden challenges of entry level work frustrating you into a dejected state?*

TRACK 8.
SCREWING UP,
PART ONE: THE
GRASS IS GREENER

At a glance: Fair enough, you hate your job. You will inevitably begin to contemplate lots of options. Make sure you don't prolong your agony.

So you've come to this place. We spoke of it earlier. You graduated, threw out some résumés and landed that entry level job. Congrats!

Yet, within a short time of receiving the position, you realize the job is not capturing your interest. It's not what you expected. Perhaps you seriously dislike it. And within mere months of getting the job, you decide it's simply not the job for you.

As a result, you slowly start looking for something else. You investigate going back to school, probe into other jobs, and even wonder about that epic trip to East Timor your friends want you to join them for. Three options that all have merit. After a lot of thought, you scratch school, decide it's not the time to go exploring foreign lands, and instead decide to take your next job. Away you go. This next job will be great!

It's a situation that plays out time and time again on a daily basis, to a surprisingly accurate degree. Give or take, this is the emerging generation's entry level career pattern that riddles the first few years of work for many, many people. In all serious-ness, on the surface there's nothing wrong with it. These are the types of decisions faced by the emerging workforce on mass scale. It is fairly standard stuff, isn't it?

Sure it is! We can already evaluate what has happened. The brick wall has been hit. Good thing we knew it would be. You just finished reading about the five major forces that make it exceedingly difficult to avoid the wall, so you can't really be blamed. On the positive side, though, you rebounded fast. You recognized that a change was needed and you faced the chal-lenge head-on. This seems fine. Three appealing options were evaluated and one rational decision was made. There is nothing wrong there, right?

Well, that's where scenarios like the one you just read get touchy. So, let's break the surface. Because it's true that at first glance this decision seems cool. A job was taken on but was quickly determined to not be the right fit. Some combination of forces caused you to hit the wall. You then made the best choice you could. You did the right thing. Or did you?

We now enter the second (short) phase of this book. We shift from learning about why the brick wall forms to understanding the fallout that occurs after the collision. The following two tracks describe the two deadly reactions young workers have after feeling the brick-smack. These are predictable responses that potentially take an entry level situation from bad to worse. What's especially troubling is that these reactions can seem so innocent, so obvious. You just read one of them. You probably didn't even notice, right? In the same way, most people who hit the wall and fall victim to the major response patterns don't notice it either. But before they know it, their career starts to take shape in a way that is counter to their intention. That's why the following two tracks are so desperately needed.

When the wall is hit, young workers react. We should expect nothing less. The decisions these workers make seem rational. They really do. But all is not as it seems. For beneath, there are layers. Layers that are worth analyzing. So, let's peel them back.

Layer 1

First, although I breezed through it, this is classic brick wall scenario stuff. Of course you recognized it. Someone gets a job and they're excited, but within a short time after tasting entry level work their excitement turns to disdain. From there, the Choice Defect takes over and the person starts checking out other options. Then finally, after due consideration, they leave one entry level job for another. Standard.

Layer 2

You are now starting to catch on that one entry level job often looks very similar to the next. Actually, they're just about identical twins. In that light, what has this person actually done? They've traded their entry level job, the one they disliked, for another person's entry level job, another person who also disliked their job. Then, both parties start anew, expecting different results. You can guess where that leads.

Layer 3

It actually gets worse. Not only have these two fictional employees done a straight-up swap, but of greater consequence, they have both erased the time they put into their first job only to start from scratch all over again. Not on their résumé, of course. They still get to write down that they were employed for a year. However, by swapping jobs these employees have erased the trust, comfort, and experience they were starting to build up with their first employer, only to start all over again. Although on paper the trade was an equal, one-to-one change-over, both people lose out in the end. Why? Because entry level employment is a rite of passage. In order to get through the passage, you must build up enough trust in the higher-ups to earn the responsibility of a next-level job. This takes time, and if you keep changing jobs, the stopwatch keeps being reset.

Magnetic allure: The "career change"

There is no bigger pull, no bigger attraction early in your career, than the desire to switch jobs. I am certain you'll feel it – absolutely certain. The very idea is much too inviting to stay out of your mind as you move through your entry level stage. I understand it. I went through it. I gave into it. But, I also now understand the effects a choice like this can have on your career. What seems like a proactive move away from a job you are not enjoying to a job that seems to have much more promise has a hidden downside that many don't take into consideration. It's a downside that is failed to be grasped because we've had the wool pulled over our eyes, time and time again, by those who gave us short-sighted career advice.

Now, I fully understand that what I'm about to tell you will be contradictory to other advice you've received, but I'm trying to remove the wool. Regurgitated advice has led you astray. It's time to see clearly.

There is a common belief, one that is echoed by just about every career counsellor you've ever heard from, that the emerging generation of workers will change careers anywhere from three to seven times in their working lifespan (depending on the report). Furthermore, these advisors go on to give the impression that this type of career jumping is a good thing and is to be expected. As a result, emerging workers are led to believe their career will, and should, be marked by a series of reincarnations. However, let me be the first to tell you that this advice is a joke. On a couple of different levels, the suggestion that you should change careers a number of times is atrocious advice.

First off, no labour observing group of repute provides study data on career changes. That's what makes the advice not only bad, but funny. There is way too much gray area in what constitutes a career change. Therefore, nobody even tracks it, at least no one worth quoting. In fact, the American Bureau of Labor Statistics (BLS) explains it this way:

> *Until a consensus emerges among economists, sociologists, career-guidance professionals, and other labor market observers about the appropriate criteria that should be used for defining careers and career changes, BLS and other statistical organizations will not be able to produce estimates on the number of times people change careers in their lives.*

So, what reports are these career advisors referring to? It's suspect, at best. The reason why no group studies career changes is because it's too hard to define what a career change is. For instance, if you shift from sales to marketing within the same company, is that a career change? How about if you're employed as a business analyst and then start your own consulting company in the same field? Would that be considered a career change? Perhaps, but who really knows? Defining what a career change is to an exacting degree is a pointless pursuit. The concept is way too ambiguous, and researchers know this.

Further, regardless of whether or not we could define what

a career change is and then study it, the advice would still be terrible advice. Why do you care how many times the average person changes their career? That's right, you don't. What constitutes the average career is not very important to your career. All you are worried about is one: your own.

But more importantly still, even if we could define career change and measure it, and even if you did actually care, the advice would still be the worst career advice that you're force fed. Any support of the notion that a career should be designed with the goal of changing careers three to seven times is dumb, and more importantly, harmful. Your career goal should not be to switch things up a handful of times... unless career vagabonding is the pursuit, of course.

Rather, your efforts should stay focused on continually aligning your current career path with the direction that will fulfill your individual pursuit of career and life success.

There are no re-dos

You only have one career. Period. It won't change, only evolve. Your career is your entire body of work. You can't change it once it starts. All you can do is work furiously to keep it in line with your life's objectives. So please, grab hold of the concept now. You have one career journey to take. No matter how badly it starts, you cannot ask for a redo. Fixes must come from you, and they are best approached by pulling yourself in the direction you want to go rather than making giant leaps that render much of your experience and network useless.

You must continually adapt and shape your career to make it match your needs. Soulmate jobs don't exist unless you create them yourself. You can bounce between jobs as much as you like, but chances are you won't magically land on a job that's a perfect fit right out of the box. Those who believe they can and who exclusively try are suffering from the first major strategic screw-up that workers fall victim to early in their career. It's the 'grass is greener' syndrome.

Of course, some believe I need to tread lightly with my advice on this topic: some would say that making a 'career change' can sometimes be the greatest choice a person can make during their working life span. Consequently, they believe I shouldn't dispel people from making this kind of decision.

My response?   Their politically correct advice is much too narrow.

I am a strong supporter of finding out what it is you want to do and then working to make it happen. If you find yourself in a position of clarity with a true understanding of the field, industry, or job you want to be in and it involves a major change, by all means go after it with everything you have. Unfortunately, most of us don't have this type of clarity. Most of us will need to design our career to fit our own goals. Therefore, if you don't find yourself in a position of extreme clarity, if you are moving from one job to another without the honest knowledge that you are moving to the industry or position that will truly help you uncover more of your individually defined notion of success, then think long and hard about the switch. Because, most likely a move like this is causing unknown harm to your career. Plus, another option exists: you don't need to make giant leaps of faith; rather, you can make career moves that don't cause you harm, rather, create promise. You do this by remodelling the role you have and bridging the gap that exists between where your career is now and where you want it to be.

The easy answer leading to the hard place

Sure it's easy, thrilling, new, and satisfying to think of walking away from a job that you hate. There is no more appealing short-term solution to the feelings of dislike or frustration towards your job. It is the ultimate Band-Aid. Yet, you must find a way to see past the short-term. When making a decision to move on or not, you need to know how to keep your judgment in perspective. Changing jobs is not a cure-all. Most likely, the job change alone will not have the effect you are hoping for.

Therefore, before you make the choice to radically alter your career in one big movement, do your best to understand the full scope of your situation.

When you move from one entry level position to another, you are still in an entry level role. Even if the new job is advertised by asking for candidates with previous experience, if it pays like an entry level job and gives you the responsibility of an entry level job, then guess what? All you've done is a swap. The job you're going to will have much in common with the job you just left.

Given that scenario, the heavy-handed message is to not change jobs just for the sake of changing. This is especially the case when it is a lateral move. Most likely it's a rash decision that is looking to alleviate discomfort, but the move has no strategy. It's a fight or flight response, and your career should not be forced to suffer because of impulsive decisions. Entry level grass is rarely greener on the other side, no matter how it looks from where you are standing. Plus, you are not alone in the struggles you are facing at work. Most everyone goes through them, so please refrain from just switching places with someone else who is feeling the same way about their job as you are of yours. Often, a new start in a new job does nothing more than change the commute that you have to the office in the morning.

Career shifts: The way forward

This is one of the fundamental beliefs of Career Design. If you want a different job, then go to work, the same work, and start altering the job you currently have. Only when the shift of your immediate job has gotten to the point where a good exit presents itself should you look to move on. The first job must have done its job first. It must have played its part. This notion is something I call career shifting and it's a much different approach than career changing. Understand the differentiation.

Career shifts are job alterations that slide your career in the direction you want to take it in. It's often a series of small movements. Lots of times it will eventually result in a change of jobs. However, stage one of career shifting – a stage that cannot be overlooked – is to alter the current job you have. This is vastly different to the career change approach where you remove yourself from one pursuit and jump into another without any form of bridge to connect the two. Career shifts are strategic. Career changes are often reactive.

Shifting is strategic because it allows you to hang on to the trust, experience, comfort, goodwill, and network you have already built through the initial phase of your career (however short that career has been). Alternatively, when you make a big career jump, lots of those intangibles are erased. And as you know, to get through your entry level stage of work you need to build up enough trust within your organization to get those above you to feel comfortable giving you more responsibilities. This takes time. It takes sticking to a job long enough to build up those intangibles.

But that begs the question, how do you stick to a job you hate long enough to build up the intangibles? Or even harder, how do you convince yourself to stick with a job you hate, especially if you don't like where the job is leading (i.e. your boss' job looks worse to you than yours)? It's tough. These are major concerns, but they are exactly the kind of situations many face.

Thankfully, there is a solution

The answer is to slide your job and career in a direction that interests you. Find the parts of work that excite you (even if they are only minor tasks), then amplify that work until you showcase the value of it to others. This is the best option you have. There are minor parts of everyone's work that are appealing in one way or another. You need to find them and grab them. Taking hold of and expanding the parts of your job you like is the way to start sliding your career.

Keep in mind, the things at work you enjoy are not necessarily tasks that fit with your obvious passions in life, rather they are simply the things that satisfy the way your brain wants to work. Sometimes you need to deliberately work to find them, but this is worth the effort. You want to find a way to get excited again. You are ultimately looking to start a pet project, or to develop (what I call) a career tangent. I'll explain what I mean in a minute. But first, let's get over the hurdle many of you are thinking about.

What the hell do you do if you can't stand to stay in your job one more minute?

To begin answering that, let's quickly summarize the situation with which we opened this track. Only, let's do it from a slightly different path. It may mirror your current – or future – scenario.

You happily got an entry level job that excited you but now depresses. Consequently, you sought out other options and found one that seems much more appealing. It's also an entry level job, and you're just about to leave your current role to take it. You're just about to make your first career change. Then, you pause.

You come to the realization that you are frustrated and only running from the reality of entry level work, not from your current job (even though you freaking hate your current job). Therefore, instead of quitting your job to take on the new one, you resolve to break through the entry level stage of work. This becomes your primary goal, more important than scratching the itch to move on. And to break through the entry level stage of work, you decide it's best to remain in the job you have in order to maintain the trust and relationships you have already started to build. After all, you haven't done terribly at your job, you've only been in cruise control. So, you decide to focus in once again.

But not all is settled inside of you. You recognize that you have tried to buckle down at work before and lost the motivation to do so within a matter of weeks. Therefore, you are doubtful of what would be different this time. You figure you need a plan. Actually, you know you need a plan. You are resolved to not let the job you can't stand negatively impact you more than it already has. So, this is what you do...

The career shift plan: Developing a tangent

This plan is not only for those who are contemplating a change of jobs. This is also a great strategy for those interested in garnering positive attention through their work. The best part is, the plan is blatantly simple. Laying the foundation is something you can do in five minutes. It hones your perspective and pursuit. So whether you are in a working situation that needs immediate fixing or simply looking to make more fulfilling steps forward, follow these steps:

Do an inventory of all the things you do in your job. (To find a template, go to the tools page at tylerwaye.com)

1. Use three different headings to take an inventory of your working situation: a) Tasks; b) Responsibilities; c) Qualities that would make me better at my job). Don't leave anything out. Cover the whole gamut; stuff you love, stuff that's mundane, stuff you hate. It should look something like this.

Tasks
   a. Respond to emails
   b. Participate in meetings
   c. Answer customer service calls
   d. Etc.

Responsibilities
   e. Make sure our customers maintain a satisfaction

rating of 90%

    f.   Grow customer base by 5% this year

    g. Cover the phones during lunch break

    h. Etc.

Qualities that would make me better at my job
    i.   The ability to network

    j.   The ability to speak clearly in meetings

    k. The ability to not get so frustrated by the annoying people I work with

    l.   Etc.

2. Now take your inventory list and place a check beside the tasks, responsibilities and qualities you have interest in getting better at. These are the things you would have interest in learning. Place an X beside the stuff you hate, as well as the stuff you have no interest in trying to improve.

3. Then find the stuff on your list that your organization has a vested interest in you getting better at. Circle those. These are the things your organization would be pleased if you became better at doing, or added that responsibility, or improved that quality. Assess this step from all angles or the bigger picture, not just within the current scope of your job.

4. Finally, scroll through your list. Find the items that have check marks beside them and circles around them. You have now found the parts of your job that you like enough to get better at and that your organization would have an interest in helping you develop.

5. Choose one, the best one. The one that excites you most. You have now found your pet project. This is your career tangent. This is where you begin to shift your job.

6. Now write it down. Mentally file it. We'll be revisiting this

concept in a future track.

I'm serious: do the exercise

Remember

The purpose of this track was to give you a good understanding of one of the major sidesteps that slows many people's early career progress: the 'grass is greener' syndrome. It's directly linked to the brick wall and the forces you read about in the early tracks of this book. They all contribute to a pressing, growing urge to jump jobs.

No doubt, the feelings bubbling up are real; I don't doubt that for a minute. However, they can also be damaging. Very damaging. By jumping from one job to the next, you are most likely prolonging your time in the entry level phase of your career, a situation to be avoided. But don't just stay the course, fix it!

Backtracks

When your job sucks, you want to find a resolution. You feel the overwhelming urge to solve your own problem. The obvious solution? Switch jobs. It's the response most people have. But heed the warning: entry level jobs are all very, very similar. There is no point in leaving a job that sucks to fill the position that was left by someone else who also thought their job sucks. The grass is probably not any greener. At some point you need to solve the problem in a different way. You need to get off the career merry-go-round.

The starting place for this new solution is to fix the current job you have. Suck all the marrow from the bone. You must find a way to re-engage and pour your energy in. Then, once you turn your current job around, that is when you can start looking at an appropriate exit strategy. But you make the exit on your own terms, at your own time. How do you figure out how to re-engage? You find a pet project. You develop a career tangent.

> Question 13. *What are the consequences of making a sudden and severe 'career change'?*

> Question 14. *At work, what would be the impact on your energy level if you could find a specific part of your job into which you had significant interest of pouring your effort and attention?*

> Question 15. *What is your career tangent? (Do the exercise!)*

TRACK 9.
SCREWING UP,
PART TWO:
SELF-SABOTAGE

At a glance: Why does it happen? If we only knew. But don't be blind to the devastating effect of self-sabotage... and how it sneaks up.

In Screwing Up, Part Two, once again we touch on a brick wall scenario. It's something you're getting very familiar with. Young, talented, bright people get jobs, are excited to begin work, and then, in a short time, start to struggle with their new reality. Those who suffer this fate make up a big group. Most likely it's a group very similar to the 46% of people in the Leadership IQ study who fail at work within the first eighteen months of starting. There's no shortage of people who hit the brick wall.

And of this large group of young workers hitting the wall, different people react in different ways. The responses vary. People break off in predictable streams. Patterns begin to form. The first response is the one we discussed in the Grass is Greener track: that is, many of the workers who hit the wall respond by frantically searching for new options (also called Screwing Up, Part One). The second pattern – Screwing Up, Part Two – stems from a different response altogether, and the behaviour it elicits is fascinating. Of course, it is also disappointing, frustrating, tormenting, and disheartening, but without a doubt it's still fascinating. The response is a pattern I started to describe as self-sabotage. I would later learn that psychologists know it by a different name.

I observed this phenomenon – self-sabotage – for years before I fully understood it. Young workers would get an entry level job and reality would fail to align with the conscious or subconscious expectations they had about work. It was nothing major that caused this misalignment to occur, just the cumulative effect of several subtle but powerful dynamics (the ones you read about in the opening tracks) presented in unexpected ways that caused troubling feelings to stir. Then, while some look to alleviate their misalignment by recalibrating their approach to work and pulling themselves forward in the most positive direction they can muster, others do something very different indeed: they recalibrate by letting themselves fail. They sabotage themselves. Not knowingly, of course, but they still do it nonetheless.

My reaction to these observations, the quick judgement, was to assume that these people were lazy or unwilling to work hard to solve the challenges in front of them (my response was the typical one). And in all fairness, it certainly would have been the accurate assessment for some of the people who fall into this disengaged category. But not all of them. Some simply didn't fit the mould. They were achievers, hard workers in other walks of life: those who do, try, and accomplish. Outside of work this group was highly engaged, but at work they were exactly the opposite. There was almost no other way to see their actions but to assume they were being lazy and uncaring. It was unexplainable, but true. Therefore, I came to the conclusion that these people were sabotaging themselves. I didn't understand it, but I kept seeing it happen.

Young people were hitting the brick wall, getting frustrated, and then actually impairing the start of their own careers. I had to figure out what this was all about. Was it possible that a large group of workers who had just started their careers, full of energy and vigour, could self-sabotage?

First things first

Hold on: before we go any further with this track, it's essential to define self-sabotage. You need to understand what I mean by this term. Over time, my rudimentary and self-proclaimed definition has become:

Self-sabotage is acting in a way that is detrimental to your end goal even when you know it's doing nothing but harm, but you're doing so because you're consciously or subconsciously trying to remove yourself from a distressing situation.

It sounds ridiculous, I know. However, I also know that many of you reading this will see part of yourself in that description. How do I know? Because I've seen it so many freaking times! Actually, it never fails to surprise me how often I witness this type of behaviour occurring. It plays out like this: you know you should act differently than you are – for the better – and although you even know how to start turning things around, you don't. For some reason, something inside you is holding you back.

If you're not already seeing part of yourself in the self-sabotage description, you may be thinking: 'That will never be me. I won't do that.' But, there is good reason to believe you will. Why do you think the 46% of the Leadership IQ participants failed at work? Self-sabotage offers a strong explanation.

The reasons why self-sabotage occurs are plentiful. Although it stems from the brick wall, the contributing causes are also things like stress, disinterest, lack of confidence, unhappiness, frustrating co-workers, lack of responsibility, lack of autonomy, etc. Yet, regardless of the reasons why, the results are always the same: you fall further and further away from the place where you ultimately want to be. It's sabotage in every sense of the word. It's also completely counter-intuitive. Why would someone sabotage their own efforts at work? Especially when so many of life's major necessities are tied to work: finances, security, healthcare, benefits, etc. It's crazy. And in case you hadn't realized, the economic picture of the world right now is not very strong. Most people have no interest in losing their jobs. That is why this irrational behaviour at work is all the more suspect. How can people possibly justify their negative actions? I had trouble believing they could.

When I first started witnessing self-sabotage, even though I was sure of the behaviours I was seeing, I had doubts. I was not convinced that people who I knew were not lazy could act in ways that were flat-out lazy. I was having trouble trusting that people who had just started work so full of excitement could have the wind taken out of their sails so quickly. I simply could not believe in the self-inflicted pain people were causing themselves. It made no sense. I was desperately seeking a different interpretation that involved anything but laziness. It took me a long time to realize that a different interpretation wasn't needed. It didn't exist. To the contrary, the self-sabotage interpretation I was forming wasn't wrong; it actually needed more conviction. It needed to be called out for what it was, not swept under the carpet. It was real, and it was damaging.

Cognitive Dissonance: The fancy name for self-sabotage

I could just give you the technical description to describe the phenomenon of Cognitive Dissonance. But rather, I'll tell you the background story of how it was discovered. It is a little more interesting.

In the 1950s, American psychologist Leon Festinger, along with his colleagues, infiltrated a cult lead by Dorothy Martin. Martin was a housewife from Chicago who had previously been part of L. Ron Hubbard's (founder of Scientology) Dianetics movement (feel free to form your own conclusions). Either way, Martin assembled a cult following around a message she'd apparently received from the planet Clarion that the world was to end in a great flood on December 21, 1954. The message also indicated that at midnight on December 20th, if she and her group followed the precise instructions outlined, they would be rescued from the end of the world by a flying saucer. It was highly convincing stuff.

Here's where the story gets really interesting, though. In the months leading up to the foretold end of the world on December 21, Leon Festinger read an article in his local paper describing this group, learned of the impending doom they believed was coming, and decided to test a theory he had begun to hypothesize. If you can imagine, he didn't quite share the same beliefs of this group. Instead, he believed he had found the perfect opportunity to test his developing notion. He had a question and a hunch.

The question: would the group have more or less allegiance to Martin and her cause after the world did not come to an end on December 21, 1954?

The hunch: after finding out Martin and her story were a hoax, the group would actually have more allegiance to the cult than they'd previously had.

How would the group react after the flying saucer and great flood failed to show up? Festinger wanted to find out, so he joined the cult.

Festinger's belief was that the group would have more

loyalty to their cause after they were forced to confront the fact that their end of the world prediction was false. Completely counter-intuitive, I agree, but Festinger believed that people who have a deeply held belief challenged by an opposing belief (or reality) react by finding ways to alleviate the inconsistency between those two beliefs. Not only did Festinger believe that the followers would work to alleviate the inconsistency between the two beliefs, he also believed that they were likely to do so in irrational ways.

So what happened?

Well, following the stroke of midnight on December 20th, the group was not picked up by a flying saucer, nor was there any evidence the world was coming to an end. Shocking! At least it was for the cult. They sat in stunned silence. That was until Martin received another message. This message offered that the world had been spared because of the great commitment and love shown by her and her following, who had been sitting around all night waiting for the flying saucer to arrive. The world had actually been saved by Martin and her group!

So how did the group react to this second message? I am sure you can guess. The commitment of the cult members to each other and their cause grew! They didn't become dejected, instead, more convinced. Their belief was not only true; it had also saved the world!

Of course, their reaction was not rational. Not even close. However, working through the conflict between two opposing beliefs does not always produce rational behaviour. Sometimes we react by doing stupid stuff. It's a phenomenon that Festinger called Cognitive Dissonance. I know it as self-sabotage.

It happens to you too

Leon Festinger's take on Cognitive Dissonance Theory suggests that when people experience inconsistency between opposing but simultaneously held thoughts or beliefs, they have a motivational drive to reduce the tension, and often do so in irrational or maladaptive ways.

The layman's version would state it this way: when you are confronted with the fact that a deeply held belief is wrong, you may react by believing or doing stupid things that make no sense.

And, the same way Cognitive Dissonance (self-sabotage) affects members of cults who are forced to deal with a flying saucer reality that differs from their beliefs, so too does it affect young people starting work who are forced to confront a reality that does not match their beliefs. We do stupid stuff. In no way does Cognitive Dissonance or self-sabotage make sense, but the beauty and difficulty of human nature is that making sense is not the primary concern.

How self-sabotage takes hold

Self-sabotage typically shows up after the brick wall is hit, manifesting itself in many ways. It can be as simple as constantly being tardy for work or taking more sick days than you should. It can be the fact that you are reluctant to speak up in meetings when you know you should, or that you always see the negative in any situation. Yet, regardless of how it shows up, the end result will always cause you problems.

Maybe not at first: sometimes you can sneak under the radar with self-sabotage for a short period of time, but it always catches up to you. Always. Hmm... perhaps in your current situation it already has. It's therefore worth thinking about.

Self-sabotage may be the reason why you don't get that promotion or strong letter of reference. Maybe it's the reason why you are let go from your job. Maybe it's the reason why you can't break through the entry level ceiling. Maybe it's reinforcing all of the negative perceptions you have about your job. It is the root cause of lots of issues you may be facing at work.

Most of the time, self-sabotage happens subconsciously. The actions are not the result of thought, only the reaction to a conflict between your beliefs and your perception of reality. You simply allow bad habits to take over good ones because you need to internally find a way to deal with the tension that developed between your job and the expectations you held about work. Before you know it, you are no longer an employee who mirrors the way you act in the rest of your life. In life, you are an all-star. At work, you're lazy and disinterested. It is not like you at all. You simply put in your time.

It sounds crazy, but lots of us do this. It is our way of dealing with our internal disconnection. Maybe you had high hopes for work and now your first job sucks. Maybe you expected more freedom and control through work, and now you have less. Reality does not match your beliefs and somehow you need to correct this. Like I said, some find a way to pull themselves up, others slide down.

See it for what it is

Self-sabotage is also easy to recognize when it is happening around you. The co-worker who is always surfing the internet... even more than everyone else. Or, the guy who comes into work like he just rolled out of bed is similarly declaring his own fate. I know you have seen it. You know what it looks like in others. It's not difficult to diagnose when it is happening around you; the hard part is recognizing when it's happening within you, then identifying and correcting self-sabotage when it becomes part of your routine. Because if you are feeling unfulfilled at work, rest assured that you are most likely self-sabotaging yourself in some way. Consciously or unconsciously, you have started to slide.

Now you may be thinking, 'You're right; I am self-sabotaging myself and maybe I could stop, but I don't like my job enough to want to change my actions.' This is typically the way we let stupid actions get rationalized in our brain. You are wrong, however, to let yourself believe it. Not that I know your working situation. I only know that self-sabotage does nothing good for you regardless of the situation. It breeds bad habits, it breeds a bad mentality, and most importantly, it prolongs your bad experience.

Reality check

Most likely, the trials you encounter during the early stages of your career are different than what you expected. So be it. You have less responsibility. You have less control. You have less vacation. You have less fun during the day. And, to top it off, you work more hours. That is entry level work. Your scenario will change, but not until you get over the hump.

Having a much smaller amount of responsibility than you think you should is not a characteristic of a bad job, it is simply a challenge to prove you can handle more. Having a role that is very restrictive in nature does not necessarily mean you are in the wrong place, it means that you are challenged to push through to the next level. And above all else, having a jerk in your department is not a reason to move on, it is a challenge to learn how to effectively deal with difficult people (because they will always be around). These are the types of challenges that you will face early in your career. They are not the challenges you expected. Unlike in the movies, you are not the person to stay up all night finishing the major strategic report that stops the company from going into bankruptcy. This isn't Hollywood. Get used to the idea that you are years away from those types of duties (if that's what you want). You see, if that is the responsibility you are looking for, you must be prepared to get through your current level first.

The other angle

How do you address the difference between your beliefs about work and the reality you face? I have given you lots of explanations but the challenge still remains. Self-sabotage occurs because of tension, and you can't just cross your fingers and hope the tension goes away. A solution is still needed.

Overcoming self-sabotage requires a different outlook. And that outlook is an appreciation for learning: learning about yourself, learning about others, learning how you interact. It sounds very 'self-help-ish,' but the solution is what the solution is.

Work is not about proving what you know, it is about learning more about the things you don't. It sounds like a small difference, but that is the different outlook needed. That's the other angle to help untangle this early career mess, and it works.

Overcoming the challenges you face at work does not go unnoticed. This is the way to prove that you are the type of employee your company wants to help develop into a bigger role. If a bigger role with your organization is of no interest to you, fair enough. However, overcoming these challenges is the only way to learn how to deal with the challenges that are thrown at you, no matter what you end up doing. I'm sorry to break it to you, but overcoming challenges is kind of the process for how a good life works. Being successful requires you to learn how to be successful, not to prove that you are.

You need to train yourself to recognize certain situations at work as personal tests. Then, find a way to take on those tests. When you are unhappy, the easy option is to find the negative. You must overcome this tendency. Seeing the negative is not the way through the spot you are in. You have tension between reality and your previously held expectations of work. One of the natural reactions is to self-sabotage your way out, but you must respond better than that. Nobody starts work in a new job with the purpose of doing poorly. Your intention was to succeed, so do your best to make sure that happens. It happens by becoming a student, by becoming an observer of what is happening around you. So, remove yourself from the emotion of the situation and investigate what is really going on.

The solution

If you were to sit down and write out a movie character who would be the ideal employee in your role, what would that character look like and do? I am guessing you know. If you were to write a movie script about a person who fixed the problems you are facing at work, what would they do?

Now write that script. I'm serious. Grab a pen and paper. Grab your laptop; get descriptive. You don't need a template for this one, keep it simple.

> *If my job was taken over by a movie character who was a raging success, they would look like this..., they would do this..., and they would act this way. Also, my movie character would be played by this actor/ actress because they...*

If you can actually sit down and think of ways to improve your situation, but you are not doing anything to make those changes happen, what excuse are you telling yourself? How are you letting Cognitive Dissonance defeat you?

Sit back, grab some popcorn, and watch your story play out

Even if you hate your job, even if you know you're in the wrong industry, why not work to your potential until you move on? If you are frustrated by the people around you, why not find a way to make those relationships operable? Prove that you can. I don't just say these things out of moral duty; I say them because this is the solution to the early career issues you face.

The incredibly ironic thing is that young employees want to do more, have more responsibility and have more freedom, but because they are not getting those things, they act in a way that ensures that they never will. They act in a way that is opposite to achieving their goals. It makes no sense. So if this is you, stop being dumb!

Self-sabotage can be either your career's worst nightmare, or it can be your leg up if you can extinguish it. Be comfortable with the fact that it happens to all of us. You need to find a way to limit it in your life. The challenges you face at work will look and feel different than the ones you have experienced in other facets of your life, including school. Be on the watch. The real challenges will sneak up on you: don't just let your situation unfold around you like you are a helpless victim. Become the observer. Sit back and watch your story play out in front of you. See it through fresh eyes. Once you can do that, finding a solution is easy.

Therefore, if work is rocky for you right now, this is your test. Find the small challenges and watch them develop. Don't let emotion suck you back in. The direction you can start to head in is a good one. We will be talking about it very soon.

Backtracks

By this point you have learned of the brick wall (and are probably sick of hearing about it by now). You have also learned of the five forces that cause the wall to form in your career. And most recently, you have learned of the two most predictable (negative) responses that occur after hitting it. The first was the 'grass is greener' syndrome. The second is self-sabotage.

Without question, self-sabotage is dumb. Makes no sense at all. But we still do it. Reality fails to line up with our expectations and we do what we do to alleviate the tension. Unfortunately, this often means we behave irrationally. So, stop letting this glitch in your brain control your fate. Now that you know better, you can do better. If you can write a script for a more successful, in-control, you, then start playing the damn part!

Question 16. Think back to a scenario when reality failed to live up to your expectations. How did you react?

Question 17. How do you rationalize your irresponsible actions?

TRACK 10.
ENOUGH IS
ENOUGH:
YOUR OFFICIAL
INTRODUCTION TO
CAREER DESIGN

At a glance: It's time for new ways forward; welcome to Career Design. Where we go from here shapes careers... and not just for the immediate future.

Okay, it's time to pull back the curtain. I've been flirting with this concept all along, giving you small glimpses. But now it is time. We launch the third and final stage of this book. You have learned why the brick wall forms, you now know how young workers negatively react after hitting it, and now it is time for solutions. So, here is Career Design; the quiet, effective, new philosophy of work that's been growing through experiments and whispers.

You know that the primary pursuit of this book is to help you successfully transition into your career. That's the top layer. But, it would be short-sighted to assume that transition is the only concern you face at work. I know that there is another issue many of the emerging workforce are facing, an issue hidden just below the surface.

Although you want to enter your career and find success, you are not quite sure you care to find success at the type of work you have encountered so far. You are undecided. Success would feel good, but not at sixty five hours a week, and not if it means working at something you couldn't care less about. As a result, when it comes to pursuing career success, you have one foot in and one foot out.

I get it. Many others do too. You are eager to do well, you want to find success, but the situation just doesn't feel right yet. (Hopefully you now have a fairly good idea of why that is.)

When it comes to your time – right here, right now – you want a career that doesn't fit a box that evolved in different times, created and still controlled by people who have different backgrounds and interests than you. That's why a new approach is needed: an approach that is created by you, for you.

That approach is the growing pursuit of Career Design, crafted in real time by those who are ahead of the curve. It will help you deal with the first part of the challenge you have been facing since the start of your career, dealing with the difficult entry into work. However, it is fully focused on the second part of the challenge too: helping you shape your career in the way you want it to start fitting into your broader life goals. So here we go: this track is your official introduction.

Where and why

In fairness, Career Design was not developed to help with the actual entry into work; that has only been a beneficial by-product. The rise of Career Design actually started in response to the second part of the career challenge that this book has been touching on all along (that is, striving to make work matter and fit with your life goals, values, ethics, etc.). There has been a growing group of people who have wanted to do well in their careers but have had no interest in doing well under the current regime of work. So, they needed another pursuit. They looked at their first option, which was to play by the traditional career rules and move forward in the best way the system would allow... and they scrapped it. They deviated. They created their own option two. They developed a new set of working principles. It is these principles, collectively, that are defining the Career Design pursuit.

Disclaimer: I am aware that by discussing Career Design in this book, I am bringing a second big career challenge into your journey when the first challenge, career entry, is already big enough. Simplicity is always greatly appreciated, but it would be negligent of me to just skip over the underlying tension you have when I know it exists. We cannot just sweep this tension under the carpet. Furthermore, the earlier you learn of this next step in the evolution of work, the faster you will be able to decide how you will proceed. That's why these Career Design tracks are needed.

So then, let us clear away the rubble surrounding your current circumstances. The major forces pushing and pulling on you, the most common early career missteps you have just been reading about, are important to know. Essential. But they offer the wide-angle view. We also need to zoom in. Your issue needs to become more granulated. When it comes to your relationship with work, a more personal conversation is needed. You need to build a career plan that does not just solve the short-term problem. You need one that fixes the entirety.

A taste of Career Design

I don't tell you this story because it's abnormally gripping or fantastically unique. I tell it because it describes the type of shifts that are afoot in the working world, shifts that include the mega-talented, of which you may be one. The shifts are happening. Silently, subtly, they are occurring all around us. Historically, incredibly talented people have been the ones destined for the upper-level corner office, committing their lives to the companies they work for. If they didn't make it, they were not living up to potential because those who were young and talented were supposed to climb the ladder. Where else could they aim? By default, there was only one direction to strive for. By climbing the ladder it meant that you were committing more and more to the organization, potentially sacrificing lifestyle for the institutional good. This was the model of work and the path of a career.

Today, however, brings a vastly different opportunity for those willing to push the boundaries of the old prototype of work. This is what Career Design is all about. But let's not get ahead of ourselves. First, the story.

My good friend Tony, an Aussie who can make new friends in his sleep, glided through school and graduated with a degree in chemical engineering. He did so while playing for his university basketball team (also playing soccer in any spare moment he had).

Following his undergraduate degree, Tony immediately went on to complete a postgraduate diploma in computer engineering. Why not? The guy has ability dripping from every pore. He completed this diploma while refining his ability to speak Mandarin and Spanish... on top of his native English (the three most powerful languages in the world). He also plays trumpet and has a passion for ripping through triathlons. I'm sure you get it; Tony is slightly above average on the curve.

But that's Tony: likeable, smart, athletic, musical, gifted with languages, and with the credentials to back it up. There are not many boxes he doesn't tick.

Yet after completing post-secondary, although Tony was the prototypical star for just about any employer in his field, he did not feel settled. After working for a short time in his industry of choice, something was amiss for this incredibly talented up-and-comer. Work didn't feel right. So, he did what many of us do, or dream of doing. He saw greener grass, got sucked in, and left his job.

Tony walked away after only just starting work and travelled for an extended period of time through places like Chile and the United Kingdom. He was young and life was good, so why not explore? Still, he knew in the back of his mind that someday life's forces would pull him in and he would need to get back to the "real world." Finally, in his mid-twenties and after enjoying the time of his life gallivanting around the world, Tony decided to go back to school in a whole different field.

...pause...

At this point in the story, Tony seems to be a textbook example of a young employee who ran head-first into the brick wall. In fairness, he is a textbook example. He came out of school excited and well-trained, then struggled to find his career footing. He felt lost. As a result he travelled, then went back to school in a seemingly unrelated field. On the surface, he was another misplaced, unaligned young worker.

unpause...

The field of choice Tony decided to go back to school for was teaching. Perhaps a little surprising for a guy who had the makings to climb any ladder he so chose. He could do anything. Teaching was his choice. Many would raise an eyebrow. And it begs the question, why wouldn't Tony shoot for the stars, big paycheque and all? He has the ability. He's an engineer with two specialties! Why teaching? It's a fair question, one he has a good answer for. To see that answer, let's go behind the scenes.

While travelling, Tony met his future wife, Colleen (a fellow Aussie and teacher). She's a gem; few sparkle so bright. It was through his wife to be that Tony was introduced to the world of international teaching. International teaching is one of those relatively unheard of employment opportunities that seem to defy the limits of how good a regular job should be. It is a job teaching the children of expatriates living in foreign countries. Sounds normal enough? Well, international schools and international teaching are anything but normal. They're fantastically abnormal. Where else do you get your housing paid for, a tax-free salary that dwarfs your domestic net salary, a chance to live in and hop between the coolest cities in the world, and fourteen weeks of holiday a year to play with? It's a tough combo to beat.

When Tony learned of the international teaching world, he made the jump. From engineering to teaching he went. Perfectly sensible. Tony wanted a certain kind of life and found the career that could make that happen.

Fast-forward a handful of years: Tony has lived and worked in cities like Shanghai and Bangkok, has travelled the world many times over, teaches fantastically motivated students, is financially settled, and still gets to coach and play his favourite sports. Talk about the perfect balance of finances, freedom, and fulfilment. Modern-day, lifestyle-based success at its best. Tony is one of the pioneers of Career Design.

From Bangkok to you

Give it some thought: Is Tony's story your story? No, but then again, you should not be looking for replicas. All Tony did was find a way to take control of his career and start earning the things he cared about earning in life. Maybe Shanghai and Bangkok are not in your cards. So be it. But the lesson that should not be lost is the opportunity to start tailor-making your career to fit the type of life that you want. That is what Career

Design is all about, and it is possible for all of us.

Career Design: The origins

Career model circa 1980 has come and gone. If you haven't fully internalized this yet, please allow it to sink in now. What careers looked like thirty years ago and what they look like today are two vastly different things. Of tremendous importance, the relationship that used to exist between employer and employee has changed. No longer is work offering people the same things it did before. Pensions and job security have been thrown out the window. Thirty years ago when you started a career, it was under the premise that if you worked for an organization for the length of your career, you would be able to retire with a nice pension that was the combination of earnings you had taken off your paycheque and money the organization put away on your behalf. It was a 'you take care of us, we'll take care or you' arrangement. A nice carrot, indeed. The idea was that if you worked long and hard for an organization, they would financially take care of you until you die. It was a valuable relationship, on both sides of the equation.

But the employment handshake no longer strikes the same deal. The vast majority of organizations are not offering pensions and job security in the same ways they did before. In fact, those employment benefits have almost become extinct. Of course, organizations are still asking for your full commitment to them. However, in return they are offering a greatly reduced benefit package. The relationship has become much more transactional. Organizations are asking you to work hard and then move on when it's time to move on, no strings attached. They are not necessarily asking for a long-term relationship, rather a limited time partnership. On the surface that seems fair enough. However, many employees have not recognized this shift. They understand that work is now a series of stops and starts, but have yet to recognize what that truly means. They still think the system of work will guide them through their entire career, allow them to stay employed, and then somehow take care of them when it's all done. Sadly, this just isn't true anymore. But by believing it is, many people are opening themselves up to be devastated by an employment market that requires a new worker mindset. It's a change that's part of the evolution of work. The only thing is, the employers have made the change; it is the workers who are lagging behind.

So, the employer and employee harmony is out of tune. You have a system of work that's evolving, but workers who are still flat-footed. People are looking to earn things from work that are no longer being offered. On top of it all, you have many organizations that are controlled by people who progressed through the old career structure and who encourage young workers to tick along in their career like nothing has changed. But lots has. You can see how fuel is being dumped on the career entry fire. As a result, you have an emerging workforce that has different needs working in a much different period of time and struggling to fit into a career mould that needs to be broken. No doubt, tension is growing. Hence the second layer of the challenge you face.

We know happiness at work is terribly low and the number of hours people are being asked to work is incredibly high. Yet, while workers increasingly become less happy and work more hours for it, what they are offered in return is declining. Something in the employment relationship has got to give. Of course, there are financial and circumstantial reasons why this relationship shift is occurring, reasons that are not easy to reverse. However, the crux of the problem remains: people are pretending the old rules still apply in a game that looks vastly different than it ever has before.

Recognition and response

What you've just read offers a glimpse into the circumstances from which Career Design emerged. The rise has been intentional, all the way. Yet, there have been no radical movements, no uprisings. Rather, Career Design has simply been the individual recognition and response to an issue by those who have seen the writing on the wall.

Career Designers, therefore, are just evaluating their employment situation for what it is. They understand the change. They also recognize there is no turning back the clock. So, instead of throwing up their hands in disgust and becoming a victim as the work world evolves around them, they have decided to change in response, with no complaints.

Armed with the understanding that job security is not what it once was, that pensions are not what they were, that hours worked are going up while happiness is going down, Career Designers are working to take back control of their situation. They have witnessed too many of the problems that result from blind faith in the system of work. They don't want to go down that path. They don't want to be a slave to their job, especially if it doesn't come with any sense of security. Instead, they want to focus on themselves. They have decided to build their skills and experience in a way that reduces their reliance on situations they have little control over. They have declared that work will be one of the building blocks of a happy, well-rounded life. They have declared that in order to remain a valuable commodity in the working world, they need to get good at something that is needed by others. And, they have decided not to chase the traditional carrots of work if that means sacrificing their life and lifestyle ideals. They are controlling the function work will play in their lives, not being battered by it.

With the end in sight

This new philosophy of work may be a lot to take in all at once. I get it. You are in the throes of career entry, potentially getting battered against the rocks. You are trying to find your footing, and this new approach to work is emerging around you. You realize you can only take one step at a time.

Perhaps the Career Design pursuit is interesting to learn about, but it's not your biggest concern at this time. Perhaps. But as I've said, this information is important to know. Remember, the early career issue you face is twofold: you want to find your footing at work, but you also want to find it in a direction that makes you happy. That's why it would not be fair to simply offer you advice that fixes half of the problem. Many of you are ready for this conversation.

So keep in mind, where you currently stand on this Career Design front is for you to decide. Is the embryonic concept of Career Design for everyone? Maybe not to its full extent. You have a long journey ahead that will require lots of exploring, and it's quite possible that the discussion of work in this track will simply be a minor blip on your radar at this time. Fair enough.

Yet, many are already toiling with these thoughts. There are certain questions that the Career Design approach to work forces you to ask yourself that are important no matter where you are in the game. The most important question is: are you prepared to carelessly let the natural flow of the masses dictate where your career journey ends? If not, then the goal, even early on, is to stop following in the footsteps of those in front, hoping it will lead to the place you want. Good lives do not work that way. Successful careers do not work that way. It's time for a new strategy.

The Career Design pursuit

Career Design is a mentality more than it is a defined road; this cannot be stressed enough. It is one part philosophy, one part practice, and in no way formulaic. As such, it is hard to define. Yet, even though the methods and progress are fluid, the pursuit is clear as crystal. And the pursuit, as individual as it is for everyone attempting it, has consolidated around a number of basic concepts, outlined below:

- Career Design is an expanding pursuit by individuals in developed nations in response to a changing work world that is throwing off the longstanding bargain and balance between employer and employee. This response is occurring with no complaints; moreso an appreciation for getting ahead of the curve.

- The main objective of Career Design is to make work, work in your life. The goal is to have work contribute to your happiness, not chip away at it.

- Career Design rests on two guiding principles: personal career control and customized success (to be described in the next track).

- The practice of Career Design recognizes that dream jobs are typically not found but created. Creating a dream job often requires continual shifts rather than huge, sudden moves (Tony's story is the exception, not the rule).

- Career Design is obsessed with getting really damn good at something that has value to other people. This is how you stay valuable in a dynamic work world that is quick to take people out at the knees.

- Career Design relies on the premise of compounding actions, basically doing something that allows you to do something bigger. This opens the door to doing something even bigger still.

- Career Design does not rest on the shoulders of only one individual; it requires developing key partners along the way.

- Career Design appreciates the importance of perception, identity, and the belief people have in you.

- Career Design is about reigniting a new sense of professionalism in which the aim is simply for good work to be done in a good way.

Where things change

Yes, this is a lot to throw at you in one track. You were formally introduced to Career Design. It should make you stop and think. Even though your career is only just starting, what are you truly trying to earn through work? What does success mean to you? Many never truly ask themselves that question, but for Career Design, that is the only question. Thankfully, this is what we're discussing in the next track.

This marks your turning point – not only in this book, but hopefully in your career. We have stopped identifying issues and started declaring new ways forward. Isn't that what you were looking for all along?

Backtracks

It has taken a long time to get here, so I applaud you for sticking it out. Also, don't worry if you are a little confused. No longer are we only just trying to solve the immediate challenge you face in your career (part one, or, career entry); we are now looking to solve the long-term problem that crops up for many as their career unfolds (part two, or, career disappointment). That's okay; this book was not meant to be easy.

Career Design is about helping you develop your career in a way that fits into your life for as long as you work, not just the first few years. This approach to work is a mentality more than a formulaic method, so the entry into your career is just as good a time as any to learn of this perspective (maybe even the best time). That's why the following tracks – the remainder of the book – will paint the Career Design approach in much more detail. It offers real solutions.

Question 18. *Why do you think people now seem more interested in shaping the way work fits into their lives than people in the past?*

Question 19. Why do you think I have offered Career Design as a solution to the career entry challenge you face?

TRACK 11.
THE GUIDING
PRINCIPLES:
CAREER DESIGN
CONTINUED

At a glance: The concepts are simple; take career control and then customize your success. Career Design is built on these two foundational principles.

The last track was only the threshold; an introduction to Career Design. Now it's time to take a step through the door... for those who are ready. This track is about Career Design's guiding principles: career control and customized success. Having said that, let's get right to the point.

Career control

Thirty years ago, organizational work was built off a mutually beneficial, long-term relationship between employer and employee. We talked about this before. It was the old 'you take care of me, we'll take care of you' premise. But times have changed and that relationship is no longer what it once was. Pensions are fading fast, employment security is a fairytale, and long-term career viability is not something you can simply expect to develop with seniority. As a result, there is a new level of responsibility placed on your shoulders to maintain control in your career. That responsibility is the impetus for this guiding principle of Career Design.

Today, successful careers require a highly developed sense to maintain value and control throughout your working lifespan. What this means is that you need to build your skills, experience, network, and mentality in a way that does not leave you susceptible to sudden change.

I say this because sudden change is just about the only element of work that can now be consistently expected. That's why control is so central to the Career Design approach. Just think about how many jobs have been slashed in recent times. Most likely you have experienced it in some form or another. Perhaps your job has already fallen victim. There are almost limitless stories of people who have been affected by the earthquakes that continue to roll through the world of work. No wonder there are so many who feel at the mercy of a flailing job market. It's a major concern. In countries like Spain and Greece, where youth unemployment is at record-breaking highs, it's growing to be much more than a concern. You must find a way to protect against the downside. For exactly that reason, today's work is about becoming resilient, and resilience is the result of taking control of your career.

Even early on, what you are trying to build through work is a package of value – skill set, network, and experience – that is meaningful to differing groups over the long haul. This takes a carefully crafted approach. You need to work hard to control your value: in order to be in a position where you truly design the role work plays in your life, maintaining professional value is essential.

I'll explain what I mean.

When you are hired, your employer is looking to have you better their position in some way. Why else would they be hiring you? They want to benefit. They want to see value because of you. Of course, the deal is not just one-sided; you want to benefit in your own way. You need to get something out of the arrangement as well. However, the benefit cannot simply be about earning tomorrow's big paycheque. It may have been before, and sure, the paycheque is a big part of work. However, today's earnings are no longer enough on their own. You see, your employer is no longer deferring some of what they are offering you until after you retire. There may not be a fat, Freedom 55 cheque waiting for you at the end of your working days (unless you create it yourself). That system of work is becoming extinct; that safety net has been removed.

What happens if you lose your job? What happens if all of your employment value is tied to the organization that just let you go? How do you recover?

Career Designers control their employment value because they understand the ramifications of the answers to those questions. They take control by building up skills, experience, education, and a network that transcends any one organization. They do this at the same time they are earning a paycheque. They view work as the opportunity to earn money, but they also view it as an opportunity to acquire and refine other personal assets. This is how the modern-day worker copes in a world where axes can swing from any direction.

Baby steps

Although control is a fundamental pursuit for those who design the function of work in their life, at this early stage in your career it is arguably not the most pressing issue. There are other things you need to work on first (e.g. how to deal with and/or recover from the brick wall). That being said, although career control should not be your central pursuit at this time, that doesn't mean the concept should be left unattended. It should be a considered factor right from day one. That is why the following tracks ensure you lay the foundation of a career that has long-term value. You may not see it now, but it is important. In fact, that importance is increasing drastically. That's why the next few tracks help you build control into your work, whether you feel the need to at this stage or not.

The remaining tracks are not just singularly focused. Let's just say they serve a dual purpose. As much as they are about helping you start to develop career control, they are even moreso about the other guiding principle of Career Design, the one guiding principle that means much more to you today.

Customized success

Career Design is about success, yes, but not any old success. Not success at all costs, regardless of where it leads. Not success that leaves people in the ditch behind you. I'm not talking about rich-guy-in-his-sports-car, Hollywood-type success. This isn't pumps-and-a-power-suit success. That's boring. No, the success we're going to talk about is customized success. Tailor-made success, where the cloth is cut just for you. It's success that pinpoints exactly what you are looking to achieve and lets go of the rest. It's not success at the expense of lifestyle, rather it is success that is lifestyle.

The anchor

Success is a term that gets thrown around a lot when it comes to careers. It is the ambiguous pot of gold at the end of the rainbow most careers try to shuffle towards. Most of us don't know what is in the pot of gold, but we are still supposed to clamber for it, right?

Not a chance. Pursuing undefined success is not the goal. Don't be swayed by the masses who have failed to figure this out. For those who are interested in a life of happiness, the word 'success' has very little meaning without context. In fact, no meaning. It's not enough to just say the word 'success'. That leads to nothing more than boastful comparisons – a waste of time. True success requires a specific target. True success is accomplishment by plan. It can't just be a hard charge in any direction. That's not success; that's ambition. We shouldn't confuse the two. Please don't confuse the two. Ambition and success are totally different. Of course, ambition may support success (it often does), but success is reaching a specific destination that's been marked out in advance. Ambition is simply a blind fury. Ambition is a race to beat whoever, however, for no other reason but to win. Therefore, you can't just be ambitious; you can't just say you want to be successful: First, you must customize it.

It's important that this point be clear. Any Career Designer's interest in blind fury ambition is nonexistent. Laughable, even. But customized success; that's different. Targeted, carefully chosen success is the lifeblood of Career Design. A fundamental objective that becomes the basis of all decisions made, customized success is the anchor that needs to be tethered to your career pursuit.

Picture perfect

We all have an idea of what success is. We see others we deem as successful and make associations. Maybe it's a

BMW? An Omega watch or designer shoes? Being vice president? Earning six figures at an early age? With very little thought, many of us tend to associate success with this sort of fuss. But that's all nonsense.

I have no qualms saying it, either. Pursuit in the direction of figures and facade is never ending. In fact, it's more of a distraction than anything else. Fail to recognize this and you're entering the blind chase. You're stuck in the old model. So, wash out the perm and shave off your mustache - this isn't the eighties. Don't follow in footsteps. Today's success is taking on a new look, and that look is particular to you.

It hasn't always been lifestyle

The shift has been fascinating. For a number of reasons, success in many parts of the world is starting to favour balance over hard charges in any one direction. This is somewhat novel. You see, instead of simply looking to earn money, prestige or influence, success for many of the emerging workforce is lifestyle-first. This may sound obvious to you: people valuing lifestyle above all else. But if we look back over history, this is a developing phenomenon. The emerging workforce is looking to earn quality of life. Period. Rarely anymore is work only about money, security, or authority. Lifestyle is the new metric making up the concept of success.

My guess is that you are part of this lifestyle-first movement. Me, too. Although many might write it off as a purely selfish pursuit, the movement runs much deeper than that. Emerging generations have seen much of the fabric of families, community, health, environment, personal time, and finances get ripped apart throughout their still-young lives. They have seen lifestyle lose its mark, so it's tough to blame people who want to make it a priority again.

Upon entering your career, success will be a notion you give much thought to. It's inevitable. You're forced to contemplate your future, and success will play its part. Knowing you're encountering the entry level years of work where it is easy to get led astray, it's vital you have a sense for the success you are aiming at, even if it feels like the furthest thing from your current reality. You still must have a notion of what success looks like. You must know what you are ultimately trying to earn through work. Otherwise you will just start making default judgments and playing follow the leader, a common mistake that must be avoided. There's great reason to think for yourself.

Faulty programming: Work doesn't need to suck

No doubt, work sucks for many of those around you. However, just because it does, does not mean you need to suffer the same fate. A career is not synonymous with a life filled with toil and drudgery. Work is not just about the daily grind or slogging through. Today, you can shape work to fit your life if you are willing to take control of the journey. If you're stuck in a spot where work sucks, if you are of the belief that work is supposed to be the crappy part of your day, change your mind. Shake off the mental chains. A different reality exists. So listen up! This isn't just fluffy babble.

Fundamentally, many of us have already set ourselves up to be filled with tension at work. We work for the sole purpose of trying to get out of work. We dream of making enough money to walk off the job. We think that life without work is better than life with work. But we're wrong. We've allowed ourselves to get wired incorrectly. We truly have. If you fall into this category – trying to avoid work – you're just throwing gas on your own flames. No wonder you struggle with work. You already believe you're supposed to. Therefore, if you are of the opinion that work sucks and it's meant to suck, you will forever remain a victim. The goal of work is not to attempt to stop working as soon as possible.

What are the filthy rich telling us?

What do Bill Gates, James Cameron, Warren Buffett, Sergei Brin, and Oprah all have in common? Sure they're richer than you can dream of, but there's something else too. Despite being rich enough to retire, have their kids retire, and have their kids' kids retire, they all still work. In fact, the majority of the richest people in the world are still active in their day jobs. Why is that? Because they're that greedy? I mean, most people dream of striking it rich some way or another in order to retire early. Yet the mega-wealthy, the ones who don't need to lift a finger, still work. What's their deal? Are they overambitious jerks? Maybe not.

It's worth thinking about. Are those people still hard-charging because they can't help but to win over and over again? Of course some are, but is there more to their story as well? Maybe these achievers who keep achieving are not the ones who are misaligned. Maybe they are not the ones missing something. In fact, what if we are the screwy ones? Why are we trying to escape work when the people who already have their cell door unlocked stay put? It's a good question. Something's amiss. But which group is wrong? The rich who still work, or the wanna-be rich who are trying to escape?

I have little doubt that those who are searching for an early escape in life are the faulty ones. They are allowing poorly thought-out visions to cloud their judgement. They are just repeating the words they've heard others speak because they think those words form the perfect strategy. They don't. You see, the goal to earn enough to avoid work is a faulty plan. It's wired to short circuit. Because, rich or not, your time needs to be filled doing something. And when all you do is try to have fun, all day, every day, it ceases to be fun. Ask anyone who's tried it.

"If you retired early, what would you do?"

I've asked this question to young grads countless times in response to hearing their dream to retire early. Invariably, the first response is travel. Following that, the conversation quickly loses steam. Why? Because they are assuming early retirement is the ticket to a life filled with happiness. I know there was a period in my career when I assumed the same thing. Yet, there are countless examples of people who are rich enough to retire early, but once they have reached that level of wealth they continue to work.

On that note, why are countless numbers of us trying to reach a destination when the people already there are telling us it's not what we think? This is part of the disconnect that exists with work. All that time in your day needs a purpose. It might as well include work. You might as well get paid.

Mark Cuban, one of the original dot-com billionaires, stated in an interview with Young Money magazine that his goal was to retire by the time he was 35 in order to travel and have time to do the things he wanted to do. Sounds pretty familiar, right? Well, Mark retired after selling his first business at the age of 32, yet within a few short years he was already creating his next one. Go figure. Life without anything to do really sucks. It may not feel that way during your week-long vacation in Mexico, but over time it does. Stop trying to have nothing to do with your time. It's not the nirvana you think it is. Time is a valuable resource that must be spent wisely; don't wish for boredom.

Today's version of success

Just imagine you had no preconceived notion of success. Imagine there was no one else to compare yourself to, or you simply didn't care to compare yourself to anyone. Imagine your only career goal was to earn the things in life you really cared about. Just imagine. How then might you redefine success for yourself? What would you aim for?

It's a fact of life. We try to do things because others have done them. We want things because others have them. It's a twitch of human nature. We want things so that we can compare. But what if you could step back for a second and get over that twitch? You may be surprised by what you discover. Perhaps the things you thought were so important are no longer so important. Perhaps the things you fear aren't so scary after all. Ask yourself, 'What if?'

I know it's a different way to think. But, it's also a different way to construct your career, where everything you do is for a reason. I suggest that that is the way you should start analyzing your decisions. The choices you face should draw back to a goal, a mission, a purpose.

It's an enticing perspective, customizing success. Thoroughly so, but I know that trying to figure out your goal in life is a challenge. Of course it is. Most likely you will not only have just one. Yet, a pursuit is still needed. In order to give you a hand, I offer the most clarifying tool I've found to help you start determining what you would like to pursue through work. You see, lifestyle-based success does not just happen by accident. A framework's needed. A plan and structure to collect and focus your thoughts is a must.

The only three ingredients

When aiming to develop a customized version of lifestyle-based success, there are only three factors to pursue: finances, freedom, and fulfilment. That's it. Three things, all needed to a degree. Everything you want in your career fits into that little triangle. Let me explain.

The three pursuits of lifestyle-based success are the pursuit of finances, the pursuit of freedom, and the pursuit of fulfilment. The three F's. Modern-day success requires all three to be present and active. That's what makes this success so different. It is what Career Designers are striving for. They want to earn, but only to the extent that it offers the freedom they want. And, they won't trade the first two (finances and freedom) if it means doing something that doesn't fulfill them. They won't settle.

Although all three factors – finances, freedom, and fulfilment – need to be present in lifestyle-based success, to what degree they are present is up to you. The dosage is for you to control. That's what makes your success a custom job. The only caveat is balance. In your version of success, you can aim for whatever level of finances, freedom, and fulfilment you want. That's for you to play with. However, you cannot give up one for the other: go too far in any one direction and the recipe gets thrown off and loses its sweetness. Therefore, success needs to be designed, targeted, and achieved. Remember, it's not the blind fury. Don't overdue one ingredient at the expense of another. That's fundamental to the Career Designers' mantra.

Finances without freedom is a lost cause. We have seen the end of that story play out many times. Lots of money at 65 hours a week is not the formula. Think of the career 'all-stars' you know who have lives in shambles outside of work. It's not a good trade-off. Alternatively, freedom without finances is a quick burn that extinguishes itself before it really gets going, a sobering reality. Without money, time can be a hard thing to fill.

Clearly, the finances and freedom relationship is well-established. If earning means you have no time to enjoy life, the model must be questioned. Once you cross a certain threshold of income (a 2010 Princeton University's Woodrow Wilson School study indicated it's about $75,000 a year in North America), increasing your earnings from there becomes less and less valuable if it requires far more hours inputted.

But what of fulfilment? Why is that a necessary ingredient? Do we really need to enjoy work? Isn't it enough to make money and earn freedom so that you can utilize them as you please? Isn't that what a good lifestyle is all about? There's a faction that says yes, it is. And at first glance, it may appear hard to argue. Money and time are major components of life. Money and time solve a lot of issues, but they don't solve one... the one there's no getting around. You only have one career and one life to do something meaningful. Money and time cannot fill that void.

That's why fulfilment in modern-day success is a necessity. It's the Godfather. When the day is out, all of your efforts add up and trickle back to fulfilment in some way. Fulfilment sees and hears all. It is the ultimate judge of success. If you don't like what you do, money and freedom cannot solve that problem.

Therefore, fulfilment must be factored in early. Work that omits it will never earn enough in the long term. Lots of money at the expense of other factors is a fallacy that must be exposed for what it is. On the flipside, a career of fulfilment that does not provide finances or freedom is not the fairy-tale it appears to be either. So, mark it in your mind now, in the new world of work: success is a balance of the three F's. Nothing more, nothing less. So to determine your unique blend of success, go to the tools page on tylerwaye.com.

Time is the gold standard

Success looks like many different things to different people. Most likely it will even mean different things to you at different stages of life. So be it. It's a moving target, but that doesn't make the pursuit a wasted one: far from it.

Success matters. It matters because life needs a pursuit that gets you out of bed in the morning. And, it doesn't matter that you may not be fully certain of what that pursuit is yet. You simply need to start looking. You only have one big ticking clock in your life, and one day it will stop ticking. When this happens, be happy with what you've aimed for. You only have a certain amount of time.

That's why time is so fascinating. It's the most valuable commodity in the world. Like magnetic north, time has a pull that keeps driving us forward, bearings intact. Therefore, it's worth asking yourself: how are you spending your time? How are you spending the most valuable thing in the world that you own?

Career Design is built through these questions. Remember,

Career Design was not, and is not, about anything more than designing your career to fit your life. That's why its pursuit has no formula, only principles to aim at. My apologies if you were expecting paint by numbers.

If you're questioning whether or not success is something you care to achieve in your career, I suggest you stop and recalibrate your definition of the word. Actively pursue your customized version. Decide what's important, target it, then start working. Not everyone will want to be an upper-floor executive of a multi-national corporation. Nor should they. Success has little to do with climbing ladders. Success looks different to you than to anyone else, so don't chase a fabricated dream. You only have a limited amount of time.

Backtracks

Now you know the two guiding principles of Career Design: career control and customized success. Together they form the hub from which the remainder of concepts you will read in the coming tracks emerge.

Control is central because the changing work landscape has forced employees to protect themselves against the downside of losing a job at any time without a safety net to rely on. It's mega-important. Admittedly, however, control may not be your most pressing need at this stage of the game. I get it. Yet, the seed still needed to be planted.

Customized success, on the other hand, is the critical piece to your puzzle regardless of where you currently stand. Customized success is a concept that allows you to clear away the clutter that clouds your career decision-making process. After you customize success, decisions get much easier. Does option A or option B earn me the things I truly care about? Simple. Without this guiding force in your life, it's easy to be led astray. Now, hopefully, we can start filling in a few more of the blanks.

Question 20. What have you noticed occurring in the new world of work that is making career control such an important factor to consider?

Question 21. Knowing that all three F's are needed, what is your mix of success? Go to the tools page on tylerwaye. com for a resource to help you map out your version of success.

TRACK 12.
NEXT STEPS: START GETTING GOOD

At a Glance: Get good at something, stay good and keep working to get better. It's the ultimate career pursuit.

At that stage in my life, it was a once-in-a-lifetime conversation. My CliffNotes takeaway? Think in terms of tools of the trade. Gain experience and narrow down what it is you really want to do in your career, then go get the tools of the trade.

The advice was so simple. And coming from Patrick LaForge, President and CEO of the Edmonton Oilers, I was keen to listen. His thoughts were in response to my question on how young employees should decide if they need to go back to school or get extra training for the career they would like to develop.

Discussions such as this marked the beginning of my interest and investigation into early career management.

Patrick's insight: "Don't make it more complicated than it is. So many young employees go back to school because they don't know what else to do. They haven't found their calling at work, so instead of asking themselves the tough questions, they simply go back to school without any real vision for where they want to end up. When you're younger, this open-ended path at school is fine. Now that you've started your career, you must choose your big moves carefully. But, don't make it more complicated than it is. Figure out what you want to do, then go get the tools of the trade needed to get you there."

Such simple advice. What kind of idiot wouldn't think of this? (Me.) But in the same breath, who does? To start work, figure out what you want to do, go get the tools of the trade, and then start getting good at the thing you want to get good at. That was Patrick's advice to me, helpful and appreciated at the time. However, little did I know the impact it would come to later have.

A quick recap

So far, if you are reading the tracks in order, page by page, you've had lots of stuff thrown at you.

First, you learned of the brick freaking wall, the shattering moment when you first get disheartened by your path at work. Almost all of us catch a piece of it to some degree. You then learned why countless young graduates still continue to run into it full speed and allow themselves to career into the career abyss.

Then you were confronted with the typical fight or flight responses that suck in many young workers. These were the tracks that explained the grass is greener syndrome and the self-sabotage curveball. Following that, you were finally introduced to the Career Design pursuit that is being developed to break the barriers on a model of work that has been asking for more and more while offering less and less.

After reading all of those tracks, where do find yourself? Hopefully with a new perspective, of course... but are you any closer to creating a strategy to deal with your day-to-day issues? Maybe you're not as far along as you would have liked. There is a reason for that. Quick solutions without the proper context typically fail to make their intended mark. Not because the solutions were bad solutions, but simply because they were not understood to the depth that was required. That's why this book has been two parts context and one part solution. However, although it took us some time to get here, we now stand on the precipice.

Emerging tactics

Although the concept of Career Design is an important and powerful progression in the evolution of work, the term is simply a term. Most Career Designers are not even aware the term exists. The Career Design concept is fluid. There is no formula. Although we all like it when situations boil down to precise equations ($a + b = c$), oftentimes, try as we might, those equations just aren't possible. Those who are developing Career Design tactics and exploring new ways to operate in today's world of work are often doing so purely through instinct and trial and error. They are essentially running experiments because no handbook on Career Design exists. Nor should it, the path can never be prescribed.

The pursuit you are undertaking, the pursuit to alter your career, is not one that can be laid out for you in advance. No template exists. The best I can offer, the best anyone can offer, is a series of emerging tactics that are seemingly giving people the boost they need. Each remaining track will uncover one of these tactics. Let them be a guiding light. For Career Design is about taking control of your situation at work and aiming at your personalized version of success. That's it. How you get there is up to you. The tactics I offer are simply making the pursuit a little more tangible.

The wakeup call

Let's go back to the conversation I had with Patrick LaForge about the steps I needed to take to further my career. I mentioned the impact his words would later have on me. Sure, his tools of the trade concept sounds utterly simple, and it is. But its message is not to be overlooked.

Sometimes people have a tendency to overthink things and clarity gets lost. No doubt we get plagued with this during the early stages of our career. The best advice is not rocket science. Before entering work, if you don't know what you want to do, just stay away from the things you know you don't want. Careers last for a long time, you simply need to avoid painting yourself into a corner. That is step one - simple. Then, once you get into work and figure out what you truly want to do, start acquiring the tools of the trade you need to begin sliding your career in that direction. It sounds easy. In a way, it is. It just took Patrick to bonk me over the head with it to make me wake up and smell the coffee. If you are in need of a bonk, this is it.

What we lost at work

For as far back as we can look, there are incredible examples of people, communities, and societies working hard to get good at very specific things, making those things valuable to others, and then prospering through the trade of their craft. It's a form of trade that is as old as time. People would find a niche, work hard to get good at that niche, make that niche important to others, then expand their working platform to a desired level that allowed them to prosper. People were craftsmen.

Yet somehow over the past couple generations of work, people seem to have lost the intention to become craftsmen, professionals, and specialists in this kind of way. The pursuit at work has shifted away. I'll argue that this is a problem. No longer do many of us strive to get really good at something specific.

Most likely, our movement away from the pursuit of getting

good at something was a result of changes that came with white-collar knowledge work. People became thinkers. They could do anything. As a result, over time we collectively fell into a trap of not aiming to get masterful at any one thing. We sought to be versatile. We could apply our brain in many different directions at a moment's notice. We had the capacity to do anything, so we did. But just like many things in life, simply because we can does not always mean we should.

Even as knowledge workers, why people ever began to fool themselves into thinking that work was not about getting as good as you could at something unique is beyond me. You work, most likely with your brain, but that does not mean you can escape the need to continually refine your craft. Success comes to those who get very good. Period. It is essential to learn to do something well, for yourself.

Getting good means learning about the nooks and crannies of a subject. It also means learning about the connections between parts that you can only see once you begin to dig really deep into a subject. It's about becoming masterful at something that others can identify you by. Get good, and then get recognized for being good. This is the way that you keep work interesting. It's the way that you maintain control in your career. And today, it's a necessary strategy; the first of our Career Design tactics. Although work has drifted from this pursuit, things are about to change. The focus on getting really good at something is about to take hold, again. My suggestion is to get ahead of the curve.

But don't just take my word. Ask the question: 'Why?'

Connecting the whys

Think back to the central reason this book came to be. It was because of the recognition that, very early on, careers split either towards success or away from it. It's a troubling reality. Troubling for individuals, of course. And troubling for organizations because it is not necessarily the people with the most genuine ability who are rising to the top, sadly, it is often those who simply show the most ambition. In fact, numerous studies (like the 2012 study conducted by Timothy Judge of Notre Dame's Mendoza College of Business) indicate that one of the best predictors of traditional career success is pure ambition. In many ways this makes complete sense. In other ways it is very disconcerting.

For the ambitious types who like to play that game, this system is fine. But what does it mean to the others who have trouble engaging in their career because a) they did not like the way the game was being played, or b) they caught on to the game too late? It often means that they missed their window of time to strive towards the type of career fulfillment and success they truly wanted. It means that work often becomes a transactional affair – about a punch card and a paycheque – regardless of whether it offers fulfillment, long-term value, etc. It means that many people need to accept a reality they feel is oh-so disheartening.

Yet, we know that for many people, this is exactly how the split occurs. If people don't find early success, they subsequently have trouble engaging in their career and then it becomes very tempting to allow work to settle into the easiest rut that it can. This is a big part of the reason why the models of work and careers have become what we know them to be. There is a small group finding great success and a larger group looking for better options. And the smaller, more powerful group is pulling work in one direction while the larger group is letting it slide in another.

Unfortunately, the power is held by those who are pulling. As a result, this ambitious cycle of work continues to prevail. It's part of our system of work, and it will stay part of our system of work – you will be governed by its rules – unless you can find a way to create your own way forward that bucks this trend.

This split, which you are getting very familiar with, is the difficult situation many have found themselves facing in recent times. The choice was to get on the fast track (even if you didn't like where that track was leading) or allow it to just fade away. Therefore, the challenge for those who were not interested in either path (fast or slow) was to find a different way to engage through work.

Therefore, the question became: how does someone stay engaged through work and become successful in their career if the rat race game is not appealing?

That's the question that started it all

It truly is. That question gave birth to Career Design. The movement only grew to have much wider implications after the fact. But, the drive originated from people who wanted to be successful, wanted to be known for doing something well, and wanted to be identified for their good work without sacrificing the bigger parts of life they were unwilling to budge on.

Yet, although the drive was clear and not overly novel (it's a drive as old as time), the answer has been difficult to identify, especially in recent times. What did these people who wanted to forge a new path of work do? Well, they looked back at how success was built throughout much of human history and they began to reenact in a modern way. They recognized that the career paths they were looking for were best discovered by working to get very good at a craft (physical or mental), making that craft valuable to others, and then developing their platform to share it.

Start getting good

That brings us back to the point at hand. The first tactic for finding early career success is to start getting really, really good at something.

This is what Patrick LaForge was touching on with his tools of the trade analogy. He was suggesting the craftsman approach to work, even for knowledge workers. He was suggesting how to recognize the area of work you want to become good at, how to start collecting the skills, how to work to get good at those skills, and then how build an identity that's directly related.

The pursuit is a mindset, much like that of athletes or artists. You pick a focus and then work hard to excel within that niche. The trick is to be interested in learning, not just in proving what you already know. Because, if all you want to do at work is prove what you already know, work loses its magnetism. If you are not asking your brain to learn new things, you are letting it disengage.

Therefore, the start of your career is about learning and then weeding through the things you do on a daily basis to uncover what you actually like doing. It's about finding those pet projects. It's about finding a career tangent that is worthwhile to explore. Oftentimes, that is how you start to identify and learn the craft you want to excel at. Of course, in the beginning that career tangent will rarely have enough immediate value to become your only pursuit. However, if the thing that motivates you most about work can be enough to flick the effort switch from off to on, from disengaged to engaged, from proving to learning, you will start to declare the type of career path you will have a lot of interest in exploring.

Think back

It's no different than the way you work at any of your hobbies. It's no different than the way you were as a kid playing sports or learning music or taking dance. You picked something you wanted to do, started to learn how to do it, and then worked to become as good as you could. It's one of the most fundamental drives in human nature. We try to become good at something and then become known for doing it. Unfortunately, we collectively bred this mentality out of work for far too long.

It happened naturally. Knowledge workers think for a living, and thinkers can be asked to think in many different directions for many different purposes. They don't operate with hands, feet, or tools. It's hard to show when learning has occurred. As a result, what started to be important got a little skewed.

Instead of being professionals who continued to learn and refine a specific craft, workers became much more interested in applying the thinking skills they had already developed.

To get your career started on the right track, to fix the issues you may already be facing, become a student again. Find out what interests you, keep learning, and help others realize why that's important. It is time to discover how engaging work can be.

A few starting places

To be fair, trying to get good at something early in your career carries with it some hurdles. By definition, it requires that you must be able to identify an area you want to get good at. This is not always the easiest thing. Also, you probably don't have a lot of control or freedom to bend your job too far away from its daily tasks. Therefore, here are a few tips to help you get started. Sometimes all it takes is getting the ball rolling.

1. Inventory List – Finding that career tangent: If you have yet to do the exercise described in the Grass is Greener track, do it. This is the one where you inventory everything you do in a day, identify the things that interest you, and then cross-reference them with things the organization has a vested interest in. This is a great way to develop a pet project and focus that excites you. You can find the template on the tools page of tylerwaye.com.

2. Professional Development: Professional development is one of the best ways to begin learning about and developing the area of work you want to focus on. Not only will you start to become the go-to person in your organization (or at the very least, be able to have conversations with the person who is that go-to person), but you will also develop relationships with others who are interested in the same things.

3. Mentorship: I recently had dinner with a successful Australian author, J.C. Burke, who has now published nine

novels. Her writing career developed relatively late in life. At the age of thirty five, working as a nurse, she had not written a single published word. How did she get a foot in the publishing door to allow her novels to skyrocket? J.C. won an opportunity to be mentored by an established Australian writer. Mentors matter.

Right next to the lost art of working to get good at something is the lost art of mentorship. Mentors can open up a world you never knew existed. It's a brilliant way to expand your skills. However, mentors won't knock on your door first. You must ask… with couth. Because, you see, if you can find a good one, a mentor will not only speed up your learning, but will also add considerable credibility to your pursuit.

On a side note – With all of the baby boomers preparing to retire in the coming years, now is the time to seek a mentor.

And just start swimming

Starting off your career by aiming away from what you don't want is the most effective launch strategy I have seen. Yet, it cannot be your only approach. You see, it's tough to walk forward while only looking back. Therefore, when working to develop your customized version of success, you must start choosing your own direction to move forward.

In his commencement speech to the Stanford graduating class of 2005, Steve Jobs told a story about the early events that gave shape to his legendary career. He said, "You can't connect the dots looking forward; you can only connect them looking backwards. So you have to trust that the dots will somehow connect in your future."

Jobs was bang-on. During the early stages of your career you have no way of knowing how your career will unfold. The best you can do is aim at the most relevant targets on the horizon and have faith that once you reach a few, you can look back and see a direction forming. Only then can you begin to connect the dots. What it takes, however, is forward progress... and that progress must aim at making you good at something unique.

Backtracks

The first step in launching a successful career is to program your brain to want to get good at something. Somehow this pursuit was lost, and it's been damaging for many people and organizations. Of course it hasn't been damaging for those who have become good at the traditional game of success. But for others who didn't like the game, oftentimes their creativity, passion, focus, and effort start to drift away. That's why I suggest you become slightly obsessed with finding the tangent in your career you want to run away with.

Finding this tangent can be challenging, no doubt. That's why the Career Tangent exercise is a good place to start. The second challenge will be developing that tangent in a way that allows/ induces others to start to see the value in it. But let's not get ahead of ourselves. We'll solve one problem at a time. So let me reiterate it: start working to get very, very, damn good at something that has value to others. This is Career Design tactic number 1.

Question 22. *Why do you believe the importance of trying to get very good at something unique began to drift away for so many workers?*

Question 23. *Other than the obvious positive impact of being good at something, what do you see are the side benefits of the process of learning to be good at something?*

TRACK 13.
HOW THE
TABLES TURN:
COMPOUNDING
ACTIONS

At a Glance: Career success builds when you do something, which opens the door for the next thing, which then brings the next big thing. Line up your actions, let them compound and tell the story that develops.

Have you ever taken the time to really think about how career success begins to unfold? Perhaps it is time you did. Let's start by revisiting Bill O'Brien's quote from an earlier track. The point he makes is a generalization, yes, but an accurate one.

People enter business as bright, well-educated, high-energy people, full of energy and desire to make a difference. By the time they are 30, a few are on the fast track and the rest 'put in their time' to do what matters to them on weekends.

This quote was written thirty years ago when Bill saw the split that was beginning to occur. What he noticed was that at some time during the early stages of young peoples' careers, their paths began to divide. Some people start to progress positively in one direction while others drift. That's not to say that lots of people don't end up somewhere in the middle, but the point of Bill O'Brien's message is clear. Everyone enters work with the energy to make good things happen, and some have their flames quickly extinguished while others find a way to make them burn brighter.

The first two thirds of this book was dedicated to discovering why people flounder at the start of their career. We were looking into why people fail. The intent was to describe why (and how) a good portion of young workers let their flame get extinguished. And rightfully so. The book has focused on failure because we learn much from our mistakes. But there is another side of the story that we have yet to explore. Sure, lots of people struggle early in their career, no doubt. But lots of people don't. Lots of people excel. So what about those who took the other path leading away from the brick wall? What about those who found success?

It's time to learn from them.

Compounding actions

Surely you've seen the compounding interest exercise in math class. It looks like some variation of this:

Q: If you invest $1000 a year from age eighteen to twenty six and it grows at 10% compound interest, how much money will you have at sixty five?

A: About half a million bucks.

Urban legend has it that when asked what man's greatest invention was, Einstein declared 'compound interest.' There's debate, of course, on whether or not Einstein actually said that, but the premise remains intact – compound interest is a powerful force. The financial world knows this all too well; it's time the rest of us figure it out.

The principle of compounding is not just valuable for your bank account. What we have failed to recognize is that compounding is just as powerful in our careers.

What goes unnoticed during the forty-plus-year career the majority of us conduct is the overwhelming influence compounding actions will have on our success. It's a foolish oversight. Success is rarely by accident; it is the cumulative effect of related actions. What this means is that success is the result of doing something which then allows you to do something else even bigger which then allows you to do something bigger yet. Like a snowball rolling downhill collecting more and more snow along the way, careers must do the same. You need to allow your actions, contributions, and experiences to compound.

This track follows on the heels of getting good at something because the two concepts go hand-in-hand. Getting good at something valuable and then finding a way to get that thing into the hands of those who value it is the most beneficial career pursuit one can follow. It is what allows you to establish career control, one of the two guiding principles of Career Design. However, it's one thing to say you want to get good at something and build a platform to do that thing on a sufficient scale, but it is quite another to actually make it happen. Easier said than done, right? That's exactly why a tactic is needed, and that tactic is compounding actions, a necessity for finding early career success.

Building a body of work

'Oeuvre' is a term used by writers, artists, and composers to describe the style and sum of their lifework. For instance, one might say "the oeuvre of Bach" to describe the collective works that best describe the style of German composer Johann Sebastian Bach. To artists, this word carries substantial meaning. Artists work their whole lives in recognition of their oeuvre. They are aware of what they will leave behind when their time to write, paint or compose has run out. They don't just work; they build a legacy. They build an oeuvre.

But why is it that only artists think about their career in this way? Wouldn't it make sense that everybody who spends a good portion of their life in a career would want to think about the collection of their work in a distinctive way? Shouldn't we all be concerned with our oeuvre? I mean: why is it that only artists carry these grander implications for their efforts? I'd suggest that maybe it's time all of us start to think about our body of work.

You will work for a long, long time. You may hope you won't, but chances are you will. At the end of the day, the work you do can either add up to a random collection of efforts or it can build up to mean something more significant. The difference comes as a result of how you approached your work from the beginning. Did you simply work, or did you do things that allowed you to do bigger things which allowed you to do even bigger things? Did you compound your actions? In the end, that slight difference adds up to a lot, just like it did with the person who invested their 1,000 bucks for a few years and is now sitting on half a million dollars.

The question is: how do you begin to compound?

Compounding actions and contributions

In school, in work, in life, wherever you are, the goal is to start doing things that contribute to the wants and needs of others. If you are unwilling to do this, throw in the career towel now. The point of work is to contribute to life outside of you. If you have yet to realize this, you are literally working towards a lost cause. You are tripping over yourself. Work is about action that contributes; and success is about compounding contributions on top of one another until they unify and start to generate their own momentum.

It sounds easy, and in a way it is. But, there is a little more to it.

Contributions are acts that happen because of you and that positively impact someone else. This is a simple concept, and right from the start of your career you should be highly focused on contributing. You should. You must. However, contributing is not enough on its own. Just as important as making the contribution is, so too is doing it in a way that allows your actions to mount on top of one another in a meaningful and impactful way. It's the way that success begins to build.

What you're seeking is a critical mass occurrence. You are trying to instigate a chain reaction. You may remember these concepts from science class or popular books. It's the 'tipping point' notion. You want to build enough contributions, one on top of the other, until those contributions get so big and loud and noticeable that people can't help but offer you more opportunity. You are trying to make something happen enough times that the next thing you know, it has become the norm.

Part one of making this happen is compounding your actions and contributions, which is vital. But so is part two...

Telling your story

Success comes to those who can compound their actions and contributions in the right way, yes. However, the compounding will never occur unless you can find a way to package those actions and contributions into a story that can be easily communicated. Other people need to learn of what you do, otherwise, how does forward progress actually take place? It only makes sense. To build success, it is imperative to have others take note of your actions. You want to make sure that your contributions can take on a life of their own.

You see, the action is the first part. You need to contribute in ways that matter, but that's not enough on its own. You must also be prepared and be able to tell the story that results from your work. Otherwise, who hears it? It's that old 'tree falling in the forest' proverb. What happens if no one is around to hear it?

It is easy to overlook this part of your journey towards success. People are not used to telling their own story. For many, it feels unnatural. It's uncomfortable. But get over it. All of the things you do in your career tell an interesting tale, so tell it. Even during the first few years of work when you feel like work is a frustrating mess, you're still writing your own story. Be aware of that story. Shape it. Your aim is to find a way to package all of the things you have done and speak to them in a way that makes your pursuit sound interesting, consistent, and relevant to the next thing you want to do.

More than any other reason, it is because of your career story that I suggest thinking long and hard about making big, sudden career jumps. I say this because the more of these sudden jumps you make, the greater difficulty you will have telling your career story in a consistent way others can believe in. No one likes a fractured story that is hard to follow.

Which way will you tip?

Think about it. In order to believe in someone enough to hand more responsibility and opportunity their way, decision-makers must trust that person will be able to follow through on the responsibility and opportunity being handed over. The only evidence these decision-makers have to help them with their decision is what they know of you (i.e., your story). And, that story will be a combination of what they are told by others, what they have personally observed and experienced with you, and what you tell them. These three factors make up the entirety of evidence they use to make their judgement call. That's it. That's your narrative. So for that reason, even from the start, your career is about writing a story. A good story. It is only through this story that you earn the opportunity to contribute in ways that compound.

It takes time, but you have time. Building this story is what makes work start to become fun. You become aware of your oeuvre. You drive to become known for something that consistently shows up through your body of work. For those who aren't working just to exercise their ambition, getting good at something, compounding contributions, and telling their story in a meaningful way is the point of work. It is the way to ensure that you tip in the right direction. It is also the way you influence others to help bump your career onto the right track.

Where the 'other' path leads

If you can contribute enough things that have value, and if you can help the story get told right, you will begin to be identified as someone who can produce similar contributions in the future. Opportunities flow to those with a track record. This will soon become the norm. It's how careers build. It's how success builds. However, the value of compounding contributions goes one step further. It is not just about keeping a list of well-documented contributions that tell a story and light the way towards success. Sure, that's the process. However, the result is much bigger.

Compounding actions and contributions is the method in which your body of work begins to grow into a cause you can be proud of. The compounding part provides the amplification needed to do it on a scale that's valuable to you and others. Storybook careers don't just happen by accident; they must be built. Slowly, over time, you slide your contributions in the direction that interests you. That's how the foundation gets laid for a fulfilling career.

Of all people, Steven Tyler of Aerosmith said it best: "You know, we're all bozos on the bus until we find some way to express ourselves."

It's true. Every career and every person starts off in a similar position. We begin through entry level work. We're all bozos on the bus. Then, somehow or another, enough of the right things come together for certain people, and in a matter of moments these people are seen in a whole different light.

How to start

The compounding contributions concept is mega-powerful, no doubt. However, it does require a few how-to first steps to get you started. Momentum needs a push. The critical mass must be reached. This is how to help your cause.

Targeting

Step one is developing the mindset that your career aiming point is always in front of you. No matter what position you find yourself in, the point at which you can connect all of the skills, experiences, and contributions you've acquired exists at a point in front of you. In terms of Career Design, I call this targeting.

Career targeting is vital because the goal is to keep a damper on the number of times you need to start your contributions over from scratch. You want your story to be as clear as possible. The main problem with jumping around in your career has less to do with the stigma of impatience and more to do with the resetting of contributions. Therefore, regardless of the need to shift between jobs that are seemingly unrelated (a situation that sometimes arises), your efforts still must be to align skills, experience, and contributions between the old job and the new one. If you don't, if you pull the plug quickly and make the move between jobs in haste, you must be aware of the inconsistency this builds into your story. The idea is not to go backwards in your career and diminish the value of the contributions you've spent years developing.

For example, if you studied psychology and want to be a police officer, don't assume you need to start over from scratch to make the switch. Find the common ground. What have you learned that applies to both jobs that will allow you to bridge the gap between the two fields?

Or, maybe you're in sales and dream of having a career in HR. How can your network support the transition?

Targeting is a mindset that pays off over time. It is the belief that the meeting point between the path you are on and the path you want to be on is always somewhere in front of you. You cannot afford to abandon the skills, network, experience, and contributions you have collected in an effort to start down an entirely new path. Even if you are certain the new path is a better one, you must find a way to get there by blending what you have done, what you know, and who you know. Otherwise, your career will look like a series of starts and stops that never goes anywhere.

Here is a simple yet vital exercise for anyone looking to make a career change that is bigger than a simple shift. You can find it on the Tools page of tylerwaye.com. You can also just draw it on paper or a napkin or whatever is within arm's reach. The twenty minutes this takes can have a major effect on your career success.

List out everything you can think of under each category and circle the things that show up more than once. Instructions don't get much simpler than that.

	Old Job	New Job
Skills		
Experience		
Network		
Contributions		

Putting up your hand

This is the second essential component, or step two, in your compounding actions strategy. And yes, it is the tip that's often written off for its simplicity. But it matters, so put your damn hand up and say, "Yes! I'll do that."

Of course, saying yes runs counter to much of the 'professional' training you receive. The common mantra today is to learn how to effectively say 'no' to people. The belief is that you must protect your time and personal workload by politely saying no to new requests. I'd be lying if I said that that concept had no merits, but it cannot be your blanket approach. The goal is to say yes to opportunity and say no to things that you are certain will only knock you off-track. Here's the kicker, though: so many of life's successful accidents have come through saying yes to something very new to you, so you must err on the side of the positive. Especially during the early stages of your career, become the person who sticks their hand up to take on a new opportunity.

Take advice from Eric Schmidt, CEO of Google: "Find a way to say yes to things. Say yes to invitations to a new country, say yes to meet new friends, say yes to learn something new."

Just try it. See where it leads. Say yes!

And don't forget to build your oeuvre

In your career, doors will be offered to you. These doors start small, but they grow bigger very fast if you can line them up. Your job is to keep opening these doors so that the next bigger one presents itself. Success is directly related to your ability to collect contributions and then tell the story.

So stay aware of the big, ticking clock. By now you may have recognized that I have a deep value and appreciation of time. I find its non-renewable supply to be a very motivating force. Take a moment to give it some thought.

You have limited amounts of time. On the flipside, you have lots of it to fill. You will be a craftsman, a professional, an artist, a something for a long period of time. Your efforts can either be random acts or they can add together to form something big. We each have an oeuvre to produce. It is not only artists who can use fancy words. We can all build a body of work that we are recognized for. When starting your career, part of your challenge is to determine where to start this body of work, but that is only a small part. The bigger challenge is developing the trust and fortitude to begin a path where you can make a series of contributions that tell a convincing and consistent story. Don't underestimate the power of compounding actions. Some people's careers split toward success and others don't. The difference is not random.

Backtracks

How else did you think successful careers developed? Fair enough: you've never really given it much thought. But, it happens like this: contributions + compounding = success. How about that for a formula?

The compounding actions concept fits hand-in-glove with getting good at something. That's why they are the first two tactics of Career Design. First, you determine what you want to spend your time and effort doing (your career tangent). Then you start compiling contributions in that direction so they can build on top of each other. Finally, you give a storyline to those contributions that can be easily understood and promoted by others.

If you are interested in building success at work, these are the initial steps. They work. And, they can be instigated from wherever you currently stand. There is a way to target a different working situation than the one you currently face. The mentality needed is one that blends your current scenario with the future one. Use forward progress to bridge the gap.

> *Question 24. What previous contribution that you were part of can you now leverage to do something bigger?*

> *Question 25. What piece of common thread can you recall from your previous actions that will begin weaving together a career story that would interest others?*

TRACK 14.
WHAT YOU THINK YOU ALREADY KNOW BUT DON'T: PLUGGING IN

At a Glance: The people you need to know, for the work you want to do, are already connected. You simply need to plug-in.

Try it. Read the following sentence and determine its meaning:

I never said she stole my money.

Simple. Now read it again and place your emphasis on a particular word, any word. Okay? How about once more? Read the sentence one more time and place the emphasis on a different word again. What did it do to the meaning?

No matter what word you emphasize in the sentence, the meaning changes. Emphasize the "I" and you infer that someone else said she stole the money. Emphasize the "money" and you suggest she stole something, but it wasn't your money. All the words work, and they each make a difference. We can all read the same sentence but get different meanings.

I therefore ask you to consider: just because you have heard something before, it does not mean you've necessarily heard it in the right way. We don't all hear the same thing. Certain advice can have great impact on some people and fall on deaf ears for others. That is one way communication gets muddy. So, when it comes to the advice you have heard in the past that has not worked for you, maybe you should think about it again. Perhaps it's not the advice that was bad, but the delivery. The emphasis was simply in the wrong place.

Meanings change with the slightest shift of weight. That's why when you come across something you have heard before, don't assume you know it to its depths. This is especially true when it comes to the principles of success. If you have come across a principle that has not worked for you in the past, maybe it's time to alter your perspective. Give the kaleidoscope a twirl.

As you can guess, I've introduced the track this way because I am going to give you advice that you have heard before. No doubt you have. The challenge this time is to find a way to make it stick.

You don't need to reinvent the wheel

When you are trying to get better at anything, the majority of gains will be made by strictly (and properly) learning the basics. That's because principles are principles for a reason: they work. Few new ones develop, and any ones that do typically require a major upheaval to get there. Yet in their quest for improvement, many people continue to seek new advice. They quickly skim over the basic principles because they are looking for something novel. They do this even though there is a good chance that all that is needed to produce the gains they are looking for is to better adhere to and practice the stuff they already know. Perhaps all that is really needed is a shift of emphasis in the advice they have already heard.

This is true for just about any pursuit you can think of. What's needed for all of us, no matter what we are trying to get better at, is the willingness to explore and experiment until we each find a way to make the essential principles (that we likely already know) fit uniquely into our lives. Whether it is our fitness, our finances, our relationships, or our career success, the basic principles are the basic principles. The goal for each of us is to find a way to make them effectively stick.

In no way is this more evident than with the career success principle of networking. We all know how important that is. Networks are your gateway into anything you want to accomplish in life. You will only get as far as those around you will allow. Yeah, you've heard it all before. However, you may never have heard it the way it will be emphasized here. The difference is slight, but immense. There is power in minor shifts. Case in point:

Woman, without her man, is nothing.

Woman: without her, man is nothing.

Networking today

This track is going to cover the success tactic of networking. As you know, it's vital. It is also Career Design tactic number three.

Few other factors come close to touching the impact your personal network will have on your career. That's why it's ironic that although we're told how important it is, very few of us are actually taught how to do it. We are left to learn on our own. Consequently, unless you're one of the blessed few who is a natural-born networker, you struggle to find a way to make this crucial factor a meaningful part of your career. This track will change that. When it comes to networking, finally, you will be taught how.

Before we get going, it is important to recognize the natural limitations of networking. Robin Dunbar of Oxford University is an anthropologist and evolutionary psychologist (whose work is well worth reading). He is known for coming up with Dunbar's number, which is the cognitive limit to the number of people that each of us can maintain stable relationships with. This number is somewhere between 100 to 230 for each person, and actually settles quite nicely around the 150 person average. That's it! 150 people is most likely the upper limit to your social relationships. There is lots of history and evidence that backs up these claims based on stuff like neocortex size and nomadic tribes, but I will spare you the details. The number is considered accurate. Your networking ability is limited. 150 is all you've got. But don't worry; I am not concerned with the upper limits of the number of people you can possibly network with. In fact, you don't even need to come close to touching it. All you need is a few, very key contacts.

I would also be remiss for not briefly mentioning the role of social networks in the discussion of networking. Many will argue that this recent technological and psychological devel-opment has completely altered the way we think about and go about personal networking: that Facebook, Twitter, and Linkedin, among others, have transported the networked world to a place from which there is no turning back. To an extent, they have. To where they have taken us, there is no turning back. However, even at their best, the social networks you know and love are only vehicles to make networking possible. They do little more than that. At best, they are simply a method, not the full package.

Introduction to networking strategy

Today, what networking needs is a plan. You need a system for reaching the people you know you need to be reaching, and that system can no longer be the shotgun method you've likely been trying to this point. Because when it comes to networking, aiming in all directions doesn't work. Unless you have charisma to burn, simply meeting those you come across without a specific objective will only carry you so far. Finding networking success in that manner is merely a product of luck. You can't afford to rely on luck. Instead, networking must be focused... and it needs a plug-in.

Tim Ferriss, the American author who exploded onto the scene in 2007 with his bestselling book The 4-Hour Workweek, provides a prime example. He was one of the first to take strategic networking and the power of plugging in to another level.

For anyone who has tried, getting a book into the hands of readers is a sincere challenge. Publishers can only take you so far. This is especially true when you are new to the industry and don't have a built-in audience. As a new author, Ferriss found himself in this position months before his first book was to launch. But he didn't sweat it. Instead, he developed a networking strategy that was centred on a specific audience and a specific number of people within that audience that he knew he needed to make contact with. Why such a targeted group? Because selling enough books during the launch to get on the bestseller lists for consecutive weeks was the goal, and this was the group and number of people to make that happen.

It was a smart plan, indeed. However, the true brilliance didn't come from the plan but rather the way in which he reached his target audience.

Without access to the thousands of people it would take to launch the book the way he intended, Tim understood that he needed to find a couple of well-connected people – plug-ins – to get his message out. The connected people he used were influential bloggers – and I employ the term 'used' lightly. In fact, he wasn't really using them at all. He just met them and then found a way to connect, make his story of interest, and then discover how he could be beneficial to them. In return, they were happy to promote the work of a new friend. It was a formula that may not have been easy, but worked with incredible success (over a million copies have been sold… and counting).

Tim Ferriss is but one example, but he shows the way in which the networking path of today has been lit with a new torch. In today's world, communities are already connected. The networks you need are already formed. Therefore, no matter what you want to accomplish, there is a group of people out there, already linked together, who can help you do whatever it is you want to do. You don't need to build a network from scratch; it already exists. All you need to do is find a way to plug-in. Understanding this places a golden ticket in your hand to accelerate the journey you are eager to begin.

The old way, looking to develop a network fully on your own, is the long road. Instead, just find the group, the forum, the organization, the community, the club that already exists in your domain and plug yourself in.

The grid has power

Like the labyrinth of power lines that light our communities, pre-existing networks have incredible power once you connect. If you can find the right plug-in, the lights will go on. If you can't find it, you may never know how close you came. Finding a plug-in is a process that sounds simple. And it is… but don't assume it's easy. There are roadblocks, and these roadblocks must be prepared for. Plugging into powerful sources requires you to overcome some legitimate hurdles. There is no getting around this. So I encourage you, when you reach these roadblocks, embrace them. Don't shy away. These roadblocks are what separate you from the crowd, like the proverbial wheat from the chaff. Without roadblocks, everyone would be networking the way you're about to.

The simple plan

Boiled down, there are three roadblocks that require over-coming before you can get plugged into a network. These road-blocks will be covered individually because they each bring unique challenges. The titles of the three roadblocks are self-explanatory, the process they cover is not as obvious. They are:

1. Finding the Right Plug-in

2. Making Contact

3. Plugging In

Finding the right plug-in

First and foremost, plug-ins are people. They are people who can get you hooked up with the communities you desire. Theoretically, the plug-in can be anyone. But, it must be someone. This should be made clear. A plug-in is a person or a small group of people. It is not the entire network you want to plug-in to. The network is one thing, the plug-in is another. They are two distinct entities, both equally important. There is a community and there is a plug-in. Therefore, finding the right plug-in is a two-part process. You must first find the proper network, community, or audience to be targeted. You then must find the person who can get you plugged in.

These two steps make up stage one of the plan. They do require thought. Finding the right community to target is essential; selecting the right person, paramount. Get either of them wrong and you chose the slow line. So then, how do you ensure your choice?

Finding the right community

When determining the community or network to target, you must ask yourself one question: am I trying to enter a community that has the power to influence me, or am I trying to enter a community that I would like to influence? Thought of another way: are you seeking decision-makers or an audience? If you can figure this out, clarity follows.

If we go back to the example of Tim Ferriss and his first book, there would have been two important groups for Tim to connect with. The first group would have been the agent, editor, and publisher who decided whether the book would get published. This group had the power to influence Tim. They were decision-makers. Reaching them would have required a specific approach. The second group was one Tim wanted to influence. They were his audience. To reach this second group, another tactic was required.

It is essential to know what you are looking to accomplish. Are you interested in reaching decision-makers or an audience? Sometimes it's both, but at different times (like Tim's situation). But once you know, selecting the right community is straightforward. Here are a couple of examples:

Trying to land the new job at your dream organization? You would be seeking decision-makers. So ask, who does the hiring? Who makes the decisions? Most likely, the manager in that department or in human resources.

How about the new album you recorded and are trying to get out to the masses? An audience is what's needed, so any place where your target audience congregates would be the community you want to plug-in to.

Finding the right plug-in
Once the community is selected, the next thing you are looking for is leverage. You must find the person or people who can help you get a foot in the door or help you amplify your message.

Sometimes the choice is obvious, sometimes not. The hiring manager at your dream organization? Obvious. The right person to get you legitimately connected to your target audience? Not as obvious. This part may take some digging as there is no magic bullet to eliminate the homework.

Who is legitimately connected in the community you desire? Are they easily accessible? Will contacting them require you to reach out to a level or two below them first? These are the types of questions you must ask. For instance, it's tough to simply email or cold-call David Foster to get a record deal. However, if David's the man you need, think about the people around him who might be able to help you get introduced. Alternatively, are there other influential people in the community who perhaps are not as well-known outside of the group but still greatly respected inside?

With a little thought, the right person or group of people to target in the community will come to you. And if all else fails, just pick someone and start there. The important part is to find a plug-in and introduce yourself in a way that captures their interest.

Making contact

Making contact is the fun part, but it takes a little work. Once you have determined the person or people you want to contact, you must find the appropriate way to connect. Today, through social media, the connection process is easier than it was ten years ago, but there is also much more clutter. You need to cut through. That's the hard part. Drop a note to Oprah on Twitter and your chance of success is less than slim. Connect by email with someone in her office, now you're getting somewhere.

Of course, the examples I use in this section are extreme. Most of us aren't looking to track down Oprah or David Foster; we are simply trying to get a foot in the door of the company down the street or the association we want to be a bigger part of. However, I use these examples to show the process for connecting with anyone. I started to discover this process when I was trying to contact CEOs almost a decade ago. It was no small task. But once you try a few times, what you quickly realize is that the people you need to reach are only people. Sure, they may have lots of time constraints and people tugging at them, but they are no different from you or me. Therefore, go for it.

In your attempts to connect, give the following things a try, depending on the difficulty of reaching the person:

- Send a message on Linkedin

- Drop a direct message on Twitter

- See if they have a blog with an email address

- Or, the one that has worked well for me: find out their organization's email formula and plug in their name. For example, the Goldman Sachs email formula is firstname. lastname@gs.com (go nuts).

Sometimes finding these email addresses can be a challenge. From my experience, the best places to look are investor relations on the website and media relations. Another of my favourites is to Google an image of the organization's business card. All of these methods have worked for me in the past, and although they might seem a little covert, sometimes you need to stretch to make contact. Keep in mind: for these connections to grow in a positive direction, you need to make the connection respectfully, so approach accordingly.

Plugging in

Plugging in requires tact, no doubt. When meeting someone for the first time, especially someone you are hoping will help you in the future, you must be smart about it. People in positions of influence have to be highly aware of the requests they get for initiating contact. First, they have an interest in protecting their time. Second, they typically represent an organization or group that's bigger than them, so they must consider factors outside of themselves. In saying that, there are still always ways to cut through the clutter.

When it comes to making meaningful contact, at the very top of the list is the requirement to be genuine and humble. Try to fake it or boost yourself up artificially and you will be shot down immediately. Coming in a close second on the screwing up list is immediately speaking to your interests and not theirs. Remember, you are approaching them for a reason; they have not approached you. Do not try to sell yourself at first contact. Instead, show your interest in them. How did you learn of them? What is it about that person that intrigued you enough to make contact? Is there something about their approach to work that is unique? Here's a hint: the reason you are contacting them should not be because they are hiring for the job you want. Potentially it is because you are interested in the management style that makes their department so sought after. Develop your reasoning before you dive in.

Depending on the situation, it may also be important to try to establish a common interest. Do they share the same beliefs about something that you do? Did you grow up in the same city or neighbourhood? Did you play the same sport or musical instrument?

As you can see, making contact in the right way needs some prior research. Don't make the call or write the email in haste and blame the other person for not responding. Give them something to hang onto. This is where your career story and your contributions are so helpful. Give them something to remember you by. Again, the success of this approach is in the details. Many people who try to connect with difficult-to-reach people fail because their attempt was a poor one. Then, they write off their ability to network. Do your home-work. Do it right. Be genuine and humble. Speak to their interests and tell an engaging story.

Flick the switch

Your awareness and ability to overcome these three

roadblocks will be a separating factor in your attempts to plugin. You already know how important networking is in your career. Now you know how to actually make it happen. So, no more excuses! If you are not the most social person, fine. You only need to connect with a handful of key people to get yourself thoroughly connected into a new community. In fact, sometimes being an introvert can be to your advantage. People will pick up on the fact that you are not just taking the shotgun approach to networking and they will appreciate your earnest effort. You simply need to get out of your own way.

Backtracks

Like most things in life, tiny shifts make a huge difference. Change the point of emphasis. Get leverage in a different place, then the thing that seemed so difficult suddenly becomes much easier. You know networking is important; there is no getting around this fact. Thankfully, you don't need to keep banging your head against the wall.

The networks you need already exist; you simply need to find a way to plug-in. How else do you expect to start making the type of contributions you are interested in making? How else will you begin to get good, really good? You cannot do it on your own. Networking may not be what you always thought it was. It's time to get plugged in.

Question 26. *To take the next step you want to take, who is the person who can best help you make that happen?*

Question 27. *How can you approach that person so that they will have an interest in your story and in developing a relationship?*

TRACK 15.
HOW THE BALL STARTS ROLLING: SOCIALLY CONSTRUCTED REALITY

At a Glance: Design your workplace identity, understand that it matters, and be active in socially constructing your career reality.

In 1928 W.I. Thomas, an American sociologist, wrote the following sentence: "If men define situations as real, they are real in their consequences."

Sexist? No doubt, but this short statement has become known as the Thomas theorem, and it nicely packages one of the most powerful forces in human psychology: the fact that perception (accurate or not) represents your current understanding of reality. It does for me too, along with everyone else.

Every day you're part of shaping the collective perception of reality. Often it occurs within and around you without a second thought. Before you know it, life appears just like you thought it would. But what if you could nudge it in a slightly different direction? Would it be possible to alter the collective perception of you?

It's time to give this some thought. Understanding the Thomas theorem can be an ace up your sleeve. The implications are potent.

When reality gets warped

In 1973 after OPEC announced drastic price increases in the price of oil, a public crisis began. Certain elements of the crisis were well-founded. For example, it was predicted that the price of oil would rise by 70%. This was enough to cause real problems and real panic, as our quality of life changes very quickly without energy. Therefore, it is reasonable to say that a number of causes of the crisis were valid. Other causes, however, not so much. For instance, one of the not-so-well-established causes: the toilet paper crisis that ensued.

During mounting fears over goods shortages, a rumour was started about the shortage of toilet paper. Why? Who knows. Nor is it important to the story. The reality is that somehow the rumour did start, and somehow the public believed it. All it would take to tip the situation into hysteria was one more ingredient. In this instance that ingredient was a casual, yet widely heard joke by Johnny Carson on The

Tonight Show about toilet paper disappearing from super-market shelves. And voila! A perfect (panic-filled) storm ensued. Many people in the United States and Japan started hoarding toilet paper like it was going extinct. It's classic Thomas theorem stuff.

Was there ever any shortage of toilet paper? Not origi-nally, but after the stockpiling began, of course there was. The toilet paper panic created a shortage that further rein-forced the fears people had about a shortage. This is how the theorem takes hold. If we define something as real, then we act in ways that make it more likely to become real. In this way, people and groups socially construct their reality.

Obvious implications

This hiccup in human nature described by the Thomas theorem is an incredibly powerful force. To a large extent it means, we see what we think we should see. It means we create self-fulfilling prophecies. Now, this doesn't happen because you are making up your observations. No, it happens because the interpretation of your observations is guiding your actions. There is a difference. You aren't making things up; you are selectively filtering. You are acting out your bias.

So know that you, along with everyone else whose actions are based on unverified observations and interpretations, are collectively influencing the way reality unfolds. Whether you realize it or not, you are swaying how the world emerges around you – for good or bad. You're an active ingredient in the shaping of reality. In fact, when it comes to your partic-ular reality, you are the most active ingredient. Therefore, adjust the interpretation, adjust the way you are perceived, adjust reality.

This track flirts with the notion of socially constructed reality for the purpose of helping you develop your work-place identity and help people to believe in you. It's a big-picture concept and also the fourth tactic of Career Design.

Some people find it touchy. They think it's gimmicky, deceptive, or fabricated. Me? I believe it is simply the way life works, the way humans work. Therefore, you can accept it for what it is or bury your head in the sand. But if you are not one to go through life pretending things are not the way they are, this advice is worth hearing.

You see, the identity you purposefully shape for yourself at work, or the identity you fall into based on the casual interpretation of others, can be one of the most powerful separating forces in life. If you can form an identity in which others believe in you as a person, a worker, a leader, then the ball starts rolling towards success. If you fail to build an identity that is believed in, the road looks awfully long and bumpy. So whatever you do, it is essential to get people to believe in you. And you can't leave it up to chance. That is why this conversation on constructing reality has to happen.

Of course, much of the process to develop your identity at work and to get others to believe in you is an organic one, no question. This should almost go without saying. Be yourself, do good work, and your identity will start to build. People will start to believe in you and more good work will start to come your way. However, just like with compounding actions, you need to start somewhere... and this can be tough. Therefore, you need to give yourself a boost. You need to be aware of this concept of socially constructed reality and bend it in your favour.

Yet, before we talk further on what to do about socially constructed realities, before we dig deeper, it is important to start one step further back. Influencing how you are perceived is important, yes. But so too is understanding the dual, and often misunderstood, power of workplace identity. So let's start there.

Your identity at work

Armed with the understanding that your career is not a short-term sprint but rather a marathon-like journey, one of your most basic career strategies should be to avoid painting yourself into a corner. We've talked about this before. But in plain language, what I specifically mean is that it is crucial to remain in a position in your career where learning, growth, and development are always at your fingertips. Otherwise, work quickly becomes more about the daily toil than it does about the opportunity and accomplishment you are striving to grab hold of. This slight difference in personal motivation is big, especially when played out over the entire course of your career. Like a pool shot that begins just a shade off, the end result can be surprisingly askew. Trajectories alter significantly, so you need to find a way to stay continually engaged. Of course, the natural questions arise (similar to the way they did in previous tracks): how do you stack the deck to make sure the good cards get dealt your way? How do you craft your workplace identity to support the pursuit of your career? How do you get people to believe in you?

They are good questions, indeed. Questions you will need to develop your own answers for. But to give you a hand, let's shed as much light as we can.

In school, your identity is handed to you and is universally understood. You're a student. The identity is clear to you and everyone else. One word, enough said. However, when you graduate, this does not remain the case; one word will no longer cut it. Take one step outside of the protective nature of school and your sense of identity takes a major blow (professions and trades notwithstanding). Given the landscape of knowledge work in which people do vaguely defined functions at work, an easily articulated identity may be tough to come by. And, it is very rarely handed to you. Therefore, you must actively craft it yourself.

But let's be fair: most employees aren't thinking about their identity. It is not on their radar. They either fail to see the value, fail to recognize the need, or convince themselves that worrying about identity is only for those with over-inflated egos. Reasonable enough. These people are entitled to their opinion, naïve or not. But as for you, I ask you (once again) to question your assumptions.

Coming back around

We have been circling around this concept, but it is now time you heard it clear and straight. The principal goal of your first five to ten years of work must be to develop a platform from which learning and doing the type of work you are interested in for the long-term is possible. All of the Career Design tactics you have been reading thus far have been focused on helping you do exactly that. Granted, this process takes time, effort, and commitment. The key, however, is to realize as early as possible that the commitment is well worth the pursuit. If you don't figure this out, the fear and the reality for many is that the possibilities we all so desperately yearn for start drifting away. When those possibilities are but specks on the horizon, they are very, very difficult to reel back in. Just look around for confirmation. Therefore, just like you need to compound contributions and find plug-ins to boost your odds of success, so too must you properly design and align your workplace identity.

Design it yourself, or others will define it for you. And, the way they define it will either work in your favour or will do exactly the opposite.

Are you believed in?

For conceptual purposes, think of your career identity as a product. It's not – it's far from it. But for this exercise, work with me.

In life, as you get to know any new product, the gut feel

that bubbles up in you goes in one of three directions.

Positive: You connect to it, trust it, believe in it

Negative: Unaligned with you, untrustworthy, a piece of crap

Unimportant: Who cares? It's purely functional, not something you are
interested in

Just like with products, the same thing happens with people and the identity you ascribe to them. People get a gut feel that goes in one of three directions. People either like that person (believe in them, trust them), get a bad vibe from them (untrustworthy, only out for their own good), or they fail to notice them in any decipherable way (uninteresting, unremarkable). Of course, this gut reaction is certainly not a black-and-white situation. Most likely, there's a larger spectrum of opinions that surface about people (and we all know views can change). However, if we were to group the spectrum of reactions into three big buckets – if we can simplify it that much – it is fair to say that two out of three of those reaction buckets don't work in the favour of the person being judged. Right? Few people want to be perceived poorly or deemed as unremarkable.

Where I'm going with this is that when it comes to your career, opportunities will pass you by if you fail to be believed in or fail to get noticed. You've learned that the opportunity to take on larger contributions comes through your track record of previous contributions, but it is very difficult to get the early career ball rolling if you are perceived as not trusted, responsible, or believed in. The faith others have in you needs to exist first.

But that's not all

There is one more reason why a crafted but authentic identity should be one of the cornerstones of your career. Perhaps this is the most important reason of all. Your identity at work is the personification of who you are and how you pour your energy into your body of work. This is not to be taken lightly. Work will be a central function in your life for decades to come.

So, what wakes you up in the morning? Is it the traditional by-products of success: money, authority, security? How about the enlightened alternative: a balancing of finances, freedom, and fulfilment? Perhaps you wake up and go to work because you've found a deeper reason to commit to the work you do. Maybe it's a cause you are passionate about. Maybe it's your desire to contribute to the community. Maybe it's your inner drive to simply work hard and make things happen. Perhaps you even love your job. Regardless of the reason, when you find a way to develop a workplace identity that complements the work you do and the person you are, the sun shines a little brighter in your office.

A little inner tension is not always a bad thing

One of the best examples of the power of identity is described by Andre Agassi. I like the example because it shows that our passion for work, if we ever uncover it, does not always come out in a spotless, feel-good story. Life is wonderfully complex after all. Agassi's journey throughout his tennis career is case-in-point. From the outside looking in, there doesn't seem like a better Hollywood story than Agassi. His success and late-stage career comeback provided the exclamation point on his remarkable body of work... but everything is not always as it seems. That's why it's so brilliant when Agassi discloses in his autobiography, Open, "I play tennis for a living even though I hate tennis, hate it with a dark secret passion and always have."

He hated tennis. For real? How could one of the best tennis players ever hate tennis? It's a good question, one with a long answer, but for now the details of that answer are not important. What's important is what he said in an interview when asked about this secret hatred:

> I think it's my DNA with tennis. It's been so embedded that no matter how much I've been through and how much it's taken out of me at times, it's part of my life. It's part of my bones.

You see, tennis and Agassi were so deeply connected that work for him, whether he enjoyed every bit of it or not, was still something he needed to pour his energy and focus into. Tennis – his work – was embedded in his identity. He simply had to do it and had to persevere. That's the magnetic pull of finding the connection between who you are and the work you do. And yes, sometimes there is a little tension.

In truth, your relationship with work may be a love/hate situation at certain times. Michelangelo suffered tremendously while painting the Sistine Chapel, both physically and mentally. In his mind he was a sculptor, not a painter. Yet, he was essentially forced to spend four prime years of his life (the best time to continue developing his oeuvre) painting a ceiling. Furthermore, the physical toil of painting above your head for years on end was excruciating. But he persevered. Why? The easy answer is that he was commissioned by the Pope and had no alternative, but that speaks little to the energy, brilliance, and focus he poured into his projects. No, the Sistine Chapel is what the Sistine Chapel is because masterful art was so deeply ingrained in Michelangelo's spirit. He just couldn't help himself.

Michelangelo was driven by creative tension. It is the same force that drives a great deal of the most passionate work the world has ever seen. It's a force we all feel to different degrees. It shows up in frustration, it shows up in passion, it shows up in desire. And I urge you, don't run from it.

Squeeze it. Work is supposed to be tough. If you have any other conception of it, smarten up. Connect who you are with what you do and the tough parts of work will be but speed bumps along the way. This is the power of identity. Take it seriously.

The cycle of identity, perception, and reality

As important as identity is in your career, you must come to accept that not all of it is within your control. People will identify you the way they identify you and this will become their reality. Lousy as that may sound, it is the way it is. Rather than fight it, learn how to use it to your advantage. Now that you see the role identity plays in your career, now that you understand the implications of being believed in, perhaps it is time to discuss the process for influencing the social construction of reality.

Can we agree that the way others identify you is merely a product of perception? Are we on the same page with this? It is important that this is clear. The perception others have may or may not reflect the skills, ability, and commitment you possess. Rarely does it. And almost never does it reflect the skills, ability, and commitment you have the potential to possess. So, don't let yourself get pigeonholed based purely on the casual perceptions of others. It would be silly to. Therefore, in order to be identified the way you want to be identified, in order to start contributing in the way you want to contribute in your career, you must work to influence the perception of you. If this sounds devious, it's not.

Although we are taught that the cream rises to the top, this is not always the case. It's the cream that is perceived to be the cream that rises. In this way, the development of your career is not governed by fate. Tangible and intangible qualities play a role. Without question, you need to work hard to possess the skills and experience needed to do your desired work. You need the tools of the trade (hopefully by now this goes without saying). However, you must also ensure your identity is perceived in a way that makes people believe in you to do the good work you want to do. Belief is a must! There are ways to help this process along. It's not paint-by-numbers, but the steps will go a long way in guiding you to build the workplace identity you desire. Just like with almost everything else in this book, the process requires a high level of personal awareness. But note that the perception of you at work can and will change for the positive if you want it to. Adjust the force, adjust the way you are perceived, adjust reality.

This advice is equally directed to those who already feel they are seen in good light. There is still room to grow. Have fun. That's allowed, too. And keep this in mind: reality may not change overnight, but changes can start to play out more quickly than you initially expected.

Crafting your workplace identity

Keep these things in mind:

Be genuine
There is no quicker way to shoot yourself (and your career) in the foot than by trying to be someone you are not. Everyone notices and it doesn't sit well. An identity can't be forced. Instead, simply highlight the aspects of you that make you unique. Take a deep look at yourself. Do you think different, look different, talk different, work different? How can you let that difference show up in a positive way? Play to your strengths.

This may take some thought, but once you start narrowing down the aspects of you that make you a special asset in the world of work, step two is to expand on that speciality. I suggest starting slow, often by simply being aware of your assets. Personal awareness is often enough to start having your assets stand out.

Take pride in yourself; expand on what makes you unique and what you bring to the table.

Develop your career tangent

I circle back to it again, because without question this is one of my favourite pieces of early career advice. It's the smallest step I know that has the biggest impact. That is why it keeps showing up in this book. It is the pet project concept, and it is the best way to start digging yourself out of the career hole you may be facing. If you don't like your job, if you don't know where to go next in your career, if you don't know what makes you unique, do your workplace inventory. Find the aspects of your job you like that also have value to your organization. Expand on them. You career tangent is a great way to develop your identity.

As small as it is, focus on the little piece of work you like. No matter how much you are struggling with your job, there will be at least one thing that intrigues you. It can be anything: building community, strategy planning, crossing tasks off a list, meeting people, getting people excited, facilitating meetings, mediating conflict, telling stories. The list of possibilities is endless; all you need to start is one.

Once you've found it, the next step is to amplify. What else can you learn about this aspect of your job? How will this new knowledge help others around you? Where could this small aspect of work take you if you got really good? Entire careers have been built on very small niches. Just about anything you can think of is the full focus of someone's career. Be certain that if you have found something useful, someone else will too. Therefore, find the aspect of work you like, learn as much as you can, learn more, and keep amplifying.

Take advantage of the power of moments

This one is fun. I spent many months experimenting with different aspects of this concept and the results were incredible. It works like this: take advantage of the moments when you know you can have an impact on others.

During the entry stage of your career, the unfortunate truth is that most bosses don't know what their employees do for large chunks of the day. It's the nature of entry level work and the reality of the workload on your boss' plate. Therefore, use this knowledge to your advantage. Although your boss doesn't know what you do for large parts of your day, they certainly do when you are together in a meeting. It goes the same when you hand in a report they will read or when you write them an email. There are moments in your work that you can identify in advance that will have a profound impact on the impression people have of you. These moments don't just happen between you and your boss; they happen all the time with all sorts of people. Identify the moment, prepare well, and leave a good impression. Simple and effective.

As mentioned, I did a lot of testing with these concepts and the results shocked me. I chose to present myself and my ideas differently and the others around me chose to perceive me differently. There was a significant and observable difference. It was a perfect case of perception guiding reality. There is no doubt it helped me clarify and solidify my workplace identity. People may not have known what I did for a good part of my day (it wasn't their job to know). However, when it came to key moments, I made efforts to be clear with who I was, how I operated, what I was saying, and how I presented myself. I prepared with foresight, knowing that certain moments offered a chance to impact. I started to vocalize and present my guiding values; others happened to take notice. I highlighted the good work of colleagues when I believed in their effort. It resonated. No doubt it was a series of small changes, but the collective impact was anything but small.

Don't underestimate the Thomas theorem

At first glance, these small surface changes can seem trivial. You may be wondering how they can add up to help you design your identity. You may question how they impact the belief people have in you and your work. But don't forget, what happens on the surface, matters. It is what creates people's perception, and perception shapes reality. Therefore, if the reality you are seeking at work is different than what you are currently experiencing, start understanding your role. You and those around you socially construct your reality. No one plays a bigger part in your reality than you.

Backtracks

It is quite silly how much human nature gets swayed by seemingly insignificant factors. Or is it silly? These gut reactions and judgements have done the human race well. You wouldn't want to turn that instinct off. In the same breath, you don't want to be fully governed by it either. You make snap decisions which greatly alter the way you perceive reality. We all do. We can't neglect the significance of that. You need to recognize the value of helping guide the perception others have of you. So, shake off your discomfort with the concept. This is career-vital.

Perception influences that way others identify you. Your identity is a major factor in the success of your career. That's why this stuff matters. Don't let the perception of your identity be shaped by others without giving it a nudge.

Question 28. Recognizing that perception influences the reality that unfolds around us and that you play a part in this, what significance does that have for you?

Question 29. Staying true to yourself, how can you highlight the unique aspects of your character to guide how you are perceived at work?

TRACK 16.
THE ART OF LIFE
AND WORK

At a glance: Don't lose perspective; your career is only in service to your bigger life. Know what is important to you, self-manage, and start discovering how to make Career Design uniquely fit in your life.

Jay-Z and Warren Buffett make an interesting duo. Perhaps that's why Forbes invited them for an hour-long dual interview to discuss their legendary success and interest for giving back. Sure, their combined appeal is obvious. They're the ultimate juxtaposition. In fact, other than the commonality of success, it would be difficult to find two figures who appear more polar opposite than the eighty-plus-year-old investor and the Brooklyn rapper roughly half his age. Yet, what transpired during the discussion spoke more to their incredible similarities than their obvious differences.

The question is: should we be surprised?

On the surface they're unalike in just about every perceivable way. Buffett, the son of a four-time Republican representative in the U.S. government, went to schools like Wharton and Columbia. Jay-Z grew up in a housing project and didn't graduate from high school. They come from two different backgrounds. They typically roll with two different groups of people and they have cut their cloth in vastly different fields. However, one characteristic draws the life paths of these two legends inseparably close, and perhaps it's this characteristic that counts most.

Both have created a personal system for successfully navigating their way through the channels of life and the pursuits of their careers. It has been their difference-maker.

Of course, with a little digging it's clear to see that both moguls developed their ability to internally navigate in much different ways, but that couldn't matter less. The fact is, they discovered how to self-manage and they have been working to master the art of work and life as it uniquely pertains to them. Success is their result. Therefore, surprise should not be the reaction that marks this story. Instead, I suggest curiosity.

The need for self-management

Near the beginning of this book – our journey together – I offered you a quote by Peter Drucker as one of the main motivators for the tracks you've been reading. This quote has been the guiding force for much of this project. Let's revisit it:

In a few hundred years, when the history of our time is written from a long-term perspective, it is likely that the most important event those historians will see is not technology, not the Internet, not e-commerce. It is an unprecedented change in the human condition. For the first time – literally – substantial and rapidly growing numbers of people have choices. For the first time, they will have to manage themselves. And society is totally unprepared for it.

As Drucker suggests, the call to arms is for self-management. This is because society is totally unprepared for the new responsibilities modern-day life is bestowing upon us. I'm suggesting that self-management needs to take on new meaning for each of us. Big meaning. Just like every organization is now screaming for innovation, every individual should be screaming for a heightened ability to self-manage. I say this because if you want competitive advantage in life, if you want to find success (true success), you've just been nudged the secret. Learn how to manage yourself. Then learn how to manage the way that work uniquely fits into your life.

This track - the final track - is about preparing you for your future. The opportunities are great. You must believe. What's needed now is to tie together all the loose ends of the tracks you have been reading. What's needed is to figure out how Career Design will fit into your world of work. What's needed is to begin your journey into mastering the art of work and life. The goal is simply to aim at the stuff that matters, and also to find enjoyment along the way. The rest? Just let it fall away.

Undoing the collar

A new take on an old term may help. We tend to think about 'professionalism' in a very buttoned-up way. To be a professional, you need to look a certain way, talk a certain way, act a certain way and produce work in a certain way. It's a very traditional view of what professionalism is. You can picture: sharp clothes, sharp minds, sharp words, sharp actions, sharp style. Professionalism has become nicely packaged. And, of course, there is no problem with wearing power suits, high heels, or delivering impeccably stated presentations. There's a time and place for that stuff. However, even though we have come to associate professionalism with outward appearances, well-packaged personas and work that gets completed in a certain way, that doesn't mean the term should continue to be defined that way in your own mind.

I say this because a new type of professionalism is afoot, one where priorities have shifted. One that embraces inner fortitude and cultivated values. One that appreciates the ability to produce good work. One that complements Career Design with incredible harmony. And, one that makes all your career puzzle pieces begin to fully form and fit.

The new professionalism

Perhaps it is time to investigate the way you define professionalism for yourself. Don't just think about what you are trying to do through work. Think about why you do it. Think about how. It's not only about the content anymore. It's also about the process. Work is the vehicle that allows you to spend countless hours in life pursuing something that matters uniquely to you. There are few opportunities that can rival the potential this carries. Work is an incredible platform. It is worthwhile to squeeze everything from it you can. Perhaps this is what Career Design professionals are figuring out.

My take is that the new professionalism emerging today values authenticity, effectiveness, and balance more than it does anything else. It applauds you for becoming fascinated with your continued interaction with work. It is about the art of work: why you do what you do and how you make yourself effective.

This new professionalism being spun out of Career Design

is created by mixing an ability to self-manage, contributions that matter and an unwavering focus on the things that are truly important to you. I'd suggest it is a concept you hold onto as you take your next career steps. The concept neatly bundles all that you have been learning about Career Design, aiming at how to make it precisely work in your life.

Making work, work for you

I opened this track by describing the interview with Warren Buffett and Jay-Z because it is an amazing glimpse into the way self-management and a well-designed career uniquely take shape. Success of the highest order was clearly shown to have come from two people with improbably contrasting starting places. That's why the interview is so brilliant. Each legend explained how they made work, work for them. In their own way, they each personify the new professionalism. Their journey was to stay true to themselves, what they were interested in, and what they wanted to become good at. Not only did they design work in their lives, but they each did so in a way that was unique.

So what is Buffett's magic? Well, one of his tricks is that he operates within his 'circle of competence': the stuff he understands with extreme clarity. It may sound like a small thing, but this discipline is a big part of his system for success. And, how about Jay-Z? What is his success system centred on? Well, as he puts it, what's important is finding your "truth in the moment." To "stick with what (you) know," and to be able to say "this is who I am. This is what I do." Maybe their approaches are not that different after all.

These concepts can sound clichéd, but they are not. The individualized principles Buffett and Jay-Z speak of are the kinds of things that greatly impact our ability to stay on course. These two moguls built a one-of-a-kind system for themselves – a personal operating system of sorts – that allowed them to accomplish what they wanted, in a way that mattered. They learned to self-manage and they became masters in the art of work and life. They did for themselves exactly what Career Design is asking of you.

Career Design is asking you to learn how to become fascinated with your career journey, not by falling in love with the fruits of your labour, but by cherishing the way in which you helped those fruits grow.

Today's life brings with it new responsibilities. Today's career brings with it new responsibilities. By now you are well aware of the opportunities and pressures. Self-management is what's required. Career Design and the new professionalism are how you let it all take shape. You will face your downtimes. We all do. The first and largest in your career comes in the shape of a brick wall. Don't get frustrated when you hit it. Instead, focus on the recovery.

Life and work do not occur in a straight line. You will experience your share of hardship and futile tangents. Be forewarned! Bumps and bruises are coming. It is for that reason you cannot lose sight of the fact that you are trying to build a beautiful thing. You are crafting your life. Your life! And a big goal is to enjoy the wonderful voyage.

But please keep in mind that your body of work is only one part of that voyage. Sure, it is a hefty part, but only one. Work must fit into the rest. Life is the bigger canvas. That is why linear pursuits for success have run their course. Hard charges that force you to sacrifice the more important stuff only muddy the paints. Therefore, in order to be successful in your career, in order to get to the point where you look back and are happy, you must paint the full picture.

The art of life and work

For as far back as we can see, human life and work have been inextricably linked. So too will they continue to be. Life has always brought with it the need for work. So, don't let the two be at odds. Work and life need balance, maybe moreso today than ever before. That balance must be determined by you. Gadgets and apps won't help. Technology is only blurring the lines, making us quickly skim over deeper issues. There is no getting around the inner strength it takes to make life mean more, be more, and contribute more.

Most likely it is starting to feel like the weight to make good things happen in your life is resting squarely on your shoulders. It is a lot to take on. No wonder your early career challenges have become so difficult. This is hard stuff. It is also precisely why, in our quest to find success, the early stage of work is when many of us begin to feel defeated. We truly yearn for one thing but get sucked down by other forces. We have the desire to live a full life and contribute through great work; other demands and life's trials just get in the way.

But you now know better. You are aware that cookie-cut answers don't exist for the challenge of work and life that your career will force you to face. No simple solution exists. The best you can do - the absolute best - is to have a deep sense of the ultimate direction you seek and a bag of tools to help you start exploring the most sensible way to get there. The journey is all you have, and the final destination is but a light to guide the way. It's true, it will never be reached. But knowing that very thing allows you to enjoy the pursuit, to be satisfied with not having all the answers, and to find delight in the process of learning. Understand that the journey is meant to be a give-and-take game with the purpose of defining its own beauty.

If that sounds fluffy and purely philosophical, fair enough. The art of life and work is in the pursuit of shaping a beautiful life. Of course, this life is not devoid of the ugly times that sneak up on all of us; rather, it simply finds a way to persevere knowing that every good story needs struggle. Furthermore, your beautiful life does not need to be deemed beautiful by all. You are painting for an audience of one.

In the context of your life, let work do its job. Work is big and important, but its role is only in service to your greater masterpiece. So pick up your brushes, look at the big canvas, and start making your first powerful strokes. Producing your magnificent piece is a function of action and discipline. Keep your eyes up and a steady hand. Aim at the landmarks that will keep you on track. We've talked about many. Continue to question the limiting assumptions that are holding you back. The boundaries are meant to be broken. It is okay to colour outside the lines.

In closing

In this way, the book wraps up with a final denouement that contemplates self-management, new professionalism, and the art of work and life. Who knew you would end up here? You probably started the journey because you were interested in some quick advice to alleviate your early career frustration. Funny. That is how my journey started with this, too. The deeper message? Well, that just started to get exposed. I certainly didn't see it coming. You probably didn't either. But that speaks to the complexity of life. You can't connect the dots looking forward.

So then, manage your choices knowing there may not be a right answer. The answer may only become right after you make it so. That's why the success in your career will be a direct result of your ability to manage yourself. It requires you to build your own approach. To learn from others, apply in your own way, and create your own path. That is what Career Design has been urging.

Finally, don't lose sight of the reason why you will spend over forty years of your life working in your career. A big chunk of it is money, but if money stays the sole reason, the forty years becomes more of a life sentence than a defining pursuit. That's why the choices you make now, the choices you make early in your career, matter. They matter a lot. It's the whole freaking reason this book was written.

Good luck. I wish you the best.

Tyler Waye

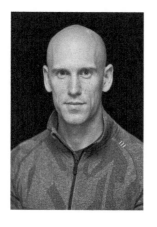

Entering work in a dream job with the Edmonton Oilers Hockey Club that culminated in a Cinderella Stanley Cup Playoff run, Tyler shook his head while voluntarily walking away after only two years on the job. Why leave? He simply knew it was not the right career path for him (something the 1700 people who applied to replace him were thankful for). Instead, he began a quest to answer the question plaguing him: "Why do so many people struggle with their entry into work?"

Fast forward a decade; mix together interviews with dozens of fortune 500 CEOs, hundreds of students and workers; a Masters degree in organizational leadership; work in countries like India, Belize, Qatar and China; and you have the body of knowledge which has Tyler rewiring our approach to work and mobilizing the next generation of workers.

CPSIA information can be obtained at www.ICGtesting.com
Printed in the USA
LVOW01s1943150114

369565LV00031B/1374/P